VIEWPOINT

STUDENT'S BOOK 1B

MICHAEL MCCARTHY

JEANNE MCCARTEN

HELEN SANDIFORD

CAMBRIDGE
UNIVERSITY PRESS

CAMBRIDGE UNIVERSITY PRESS
Cambridge, New York, Melbourne, Madrid, Cape Town,
Singapore, São Paulo, Delhi, Tokyo, Mexico City

Cambridge University Press
32 Avenue of the Americas, New York, NY 10013-2473, USA

www.cambridge.org
Information on this title: www.cambridge.org/9781107601529

First published 2012

Printed in Hong Kong, China, by Golden Cup Printing Company Limited

A catalog record for this publication is available from the British Library.

ISBN 978-0-521-13186-5 Student's Book 1
ISBN 978-1-107-60151-2 Student's Book 1A
ISBN 978-1-107-60152-9 Student's Book 1B
ISBN 978-1-107-60277-9 Workbook 1
ISBN 978-1-107-60278-6 Workbook 1A
ISBN 978-1-107-60279-3 Workbook 1B
ISBN 978-1-107-60153-6 Teacher's Edition 1
ISBN 978-1-107-63988-1 Classroom Audio 1
ISBN 978-1-107-62978-3 Classware 1

Cover and interior design: Page 2, LLC
Layout/design services and photo research: Cenveo Publisher Services/Nesbitt Graphics, Inc.
Audio production: New York Audio Productions

Authors' acknowledgements

The authors would like to thank the entire team of professionals who have contributed their expertise to creating *Viewpoint 1*. We appreciate you all, including those we have not met. Here we would like to thank the people with whom we have had the most personal, day-to-day contact through the project. In particular, Bryan Fletcher for his incredible vision, publishing ability, and drive – we deeply appreciate his confidence in us and our work; Sarah Cole, for her extraordinary editorial flair, market knowledge, technical skills, and superb direction of the project; Mary Vaughn for her usual outstandingly perceptive comments on our drafts and her excellent contributions to the material; Desmond O'Sullivan for his skills in managing the project successfully with unfailing good humor; Karen Davy for her tireless attention to detail; Catherine Black for her invaluable and timely help in the proofing stages; Graham Skerritt and Sabina Sahni for their detailed editorial comments; Dawn Elwell for her flawless design and production skills and especially her never-ending patience; Ellen Shaw for sharing her expertise so generously and for her continued support, which we value; Lorraine Poulter for her assiduous and supportive role in the creation of the Workbook; Sue Aldcorn for her work on creating the Teacher's Edition; Peter Satchell for his careful editorial support; Lisa Hutchins for making the audio program happen; Rachel Sinden for her role in setting up the online component. Carol-June Cassidy for her meticulous work with the wordlists; Tyler Heacock and Kathleen Corley, and their friends and family for the recordings they made, which fed into the materials; Ann Fiddes and Claire Dembry for their corpus support; Andrew Caines for corpus research support; Mike Boyle for contributing the articles in Units 4 and 7; Melissa Good for arranging access to the English Profile wordlists; Jenna Leonard, Sarah Quayle, and Helen Morris for making all kinds of things happen; Dr. Leo Cheng and Mercy Ships for the interview and photographs in Unit 5; Chris Waddell for the interview and photographs in Unit 12.

We would also like to express our appreciation to Hanri Pieterse and Janet Aitchison for their continued support.

Finally, we would like to thank each other for getting through another project together! In addition, Helen Sandiford would like to thank her husband, Bryan, and her daughters, Teia and Eryn, for their unwavering support.

In addition, a great number of people contributed to the research and development of *Viewpoint*. The authors and publishers would like to extend their particular thanks to the following for their valuable insights and suggestions.

Reviewers and consultants:
Elisa Borges and Samara Camilo Tomé Costa from **Instituto Brasil-Estados Unidos**, Rio de Janeiro, Brazil; Deborah Iddon from **Harmon Hall** Cuajimalpa, México; and Chris Sol Cruz from **Suncross Media LLC**. Special thanks to Sedat Cilingir, Didem Mutçalıoğlu, and Burcu Tezvan from **İstanbul Bilgi Üniversitesi**, İstanbul, Turkey for their invaluable input in reviewing both the Student's Book and Workbook.

The authors and publishers would also like to thank additional members of the editorial team: John Hicks, Lori Solbakken, and our **design** and **production** teams at Nesbitt Graphics, Inc., Page 2, LLC and New York Audio Productions.

Thank you to the models as well as all those who allowed us to use their homes and businesses for our Lesson C photographs, especially Nina Hefez; Tokyo Eat, the restaurant at the Palais de Tokyo, Paris, France; Panam Café, Paris, France; Thanksgiving grocery store, Paris, France; and Majestic Bastille Cinéma, Paris, France. Special thanks to the photographer, Fabrice Malzieu, for his skill, direction and good humor.

*And these Cambridge University Press **staff** and **advisors**:*
Mary Lousie Baez, Jeff Chen, Seil Choi, Vincent Di Blasi, Julian Eynon, Maiza Fatureto, Keiko Hirano, Chris Hughes, Peter Holly, Tomomi Katsuki, Jeff Krum, Christine Lee, John Letcher, Vicky Lin, Hugo Loyola, Joao Madureira, Alejandro Martinez, Mary McKeon, Daniela A. Meyer, Devrim Ozdemir, Jinhee Park, Gabriela Perez, Panthipa Rojanasuworapong, Luiz Rose, Howard Siegelman, Satoko Shimoyama, Ian Sutherland, Alicione Soares Tavares, Frank Vargas, Julie Watson, Irene Yang, Jess Zhou, Frank Zhu.

Viewpoint Level 1 *Scope and sequence*

	Functions / Topics	Grammar	Vocabulary	Conversation strategies	Speaking naturally
Unit 7 **Getting along** pages 74–83	• Talk about getting along with friends and family • Compare experiences of growing up in different types of families • Share views on dealing with difficult friends	• Use phrasal verbs • Use infinitives and -ing forms after adjectives, nouns, and pronouns	• Phrasal verbs on the topic of house rules (*have friends over*) • Idiomatic expressions (*drive your friends away, tag along with someone*)	• Make your meaning clear with expressions like *What I'm saying is* and *I mean* • Use expressions such as *I have to say* to show that you want to make a strong point	• Conversational expressions *page 141*
Unit 8 **Food science** pages 84–93	• Talk about farming, food, and nutrition • Share ideas for eating a healthy diet • React to statistics	• Use the passive to focus on information when talking about the past, present, and future • Use complements of verbs that describe causes and effects	• Human body parts and processes (*heart, metabolism*) • Noun and verb forms of the same root (*discovery, discover*)	• Use rhetorical questions to make a point • Give examples with expressions such as *such as, like, take,* and *for instance*	• Strong and weak forms of prepositions *page 141*
Unit 9 **Success and happiness** pages 94–103	• Define and discuss success and happiness • Share stories about happy moments and times when things went wrong	• Use the determiners *all, both, each, every, neither, none of, no* • Use -ing forms as reduced relative clauses, to describe simultaneous events, and as subjects and objects	• Expressions with *get* (*get off the ground, get under way, get off to a good start*) • Synonyms (*study = analyze*)	• Use expressions like *As far as (success) is concerned* to focus in on a topic • Use expressions like *As far as I'm concerned / can tell* to give and soften opinions	• Stress in expressions *page 142*
Checkpoint 3 Units 7–9 pages 104–105					

Listening	Reading	Writing	Vocabulary notebook	Grammar extra
My worst roommate • Four people talk about their negative experiences with roommates *"Boomerang" kids* • Two parents talk about their "boomerang" children – grown children who move back home	*Now That I've Driven All My Friends Away, I Finally Have Time For Me!* • A satirical article with suggestions for ways to get rid of friends and make time for yourself	• Write an introduction to an essay about whether family relationships are more important than friendships • Use a thesis statement • Use *what* clauses to give the most important information • Avoid errors with subjects	*Look forward to it!* • When you learn a new expression, use it in a true sentence about someone you know	• Objects with separable phrasal verbs • Phrasal verbs followed by the *-ing* form of the verb • More patterns with infinitives and *it* clauses *pages 156–157*
A food revolution! • Two radio show hosts and five listeners talk about the British chef Jamie Oliver *Backyard beekeeping* • A man talks to an interviewer about his unusual hobby – beekeeping	*Where did all the bees go?* • An article about "colony-collapse disorder" and why the disappearance of bees is a serious threat to the world's food supply	• Write a report about trends, using information in graphs and charts • Use prepositions after verbs and nouns • Use expressions for approximate numbers • Avoid errors with *fall, rise* and *grow*	*Picture this!* • Create a picture dictionary on your computer	• Question forms in the passive • Verb + object + infinitive • More verb patterns *pages 158–159*
Happy moments gone wrong! • Three people talk about happy occasions and the things that went wrong *Happiness and the community* • A sociology professor lectures on policies that can make communities happier	*Unhappy? Maybe you're not in the right country!* • An article describing ways that governments can take responsibility for their citizens' happiness	• Write a paragraph for an essay about whether governments are responsible for citizens' happiness • Use expressions to add ideas • Avoid errors with *in addition to*, etc.	*Get started!* • When you learn a new expression, imagine using it in an everyday situation. Write the situation and what you would say	• Singular or plural verbs with determiners • Determiners with and without *of* • Verbs followed by an *-ing* form or an infinitive • Verbs of perception + object + base form or *-ing* form *pages 160–161*

Checkpoint 3 Units 7–9   pages 104–105

	Functions / Topics	Grammar	Vocabulary	Conversation strategies	Speaking naturally
Unit 10 **Going places** pages 106–115	• Describe travel and vacation experiences • Report conversations • Share views on what to take on trips • Discuss the effects of tourism	• Use reported speech to report statements • Use reported speech to report questions and instructions	• Adjectives ending -ed and -ing (*amazed, amazing*) • Synonyms (*industries, businesses*)	• Use expressions such as *you mean, so what you're saying is*, and *so I guess* when drawing conclusions • Ask for more details about someone's ideas or opinions, using *In what way?*	• Silent vowels *page 142*
Unit 11 **Culture** pages 116–125	• Talk about weddings, gifts, and other traditions • Discuss the positive and negative aspects of globalization	• Use relative clauses with *when, where,* and *whose* • Use verbs with direct and indirect objects	• Expressions to describe wedding customs (*bride, walk down the aisle*) • Opposites (*loss ≠ preservation*)	• Soften your comments with expressions like *kind of, a little,* and *not really* • Use *Yeah, no* to agree with someone and then make a comment of your own	• Consonant groups *page 143*
Unit 12 **Ability** pages 126–135	• Talk about intelligence, skills, and abilities • Discuss views on parents' and teachers' roles in developing children's talents	• Use adverbs before adjectives and adverbs • Use *as . . . as* and comparative and superlative adjectives and adverbs	• Expressions to describe types of intelligence and abilities (*linguistic, articulate*) • Collocations (*raise awareness*)	• Use vague expressions like *and that kind of thing* when you don't need to be precise • Show that you strongly agree with someone, using *No doubt*	• Stress and intonation *page 143*

Checkpoint 4 Units 10–12   pages 136–137

Listening	Reading	Writing	Vocabulary notebook	Grammar extra
More adventures in Bolivia • A woman tells a friend about her plans for a trip to Bolivia *Responsible tourism* • An eco-tour guide discusses things people can do to be responsible tourists	*The tourist threat* • An article about the benefits and dangers of the tourist industry	• Write a survey article for a student magazine • Contrast ideas • Avoid errors with *although*	*So amazing!* • When you learn a new word, make word forks with other words in the same family	• Reported speech: verbs and pronouns • Reported speech: time and place expressions • Other reporting verbs • Reporting verb forms *pages 162–163*
Gift giving around the world • An interview about certain gifts in different cultures *Reviving a dying language* • Students and their professor discuss ideas for saving endangered languages	*Are we losing our culture?* • An article discussing the different aspects of culture and things that can threaten it	• Write a concluding paragraph in an essay about the effects of globalization on culture • Explain cause and effect • Avoid errors with *due to*	*Wedding bells!* • Write new vocabulary on word webs	• More on relative clauses • Prepositions in relative clauses • More on verb + direct object + prepositional phrase • Passive sentences *pages 164–165*
Minds for the future • Two friends discuss an article about the five minds that Howard Gardner identified *The genius in all of us* • Two radio show hosts talk about natural talent and giftedness	*Seeing things in a completely different way . . .* • An interview with Chris Waddell, whose disability didn't stop him from becoming a world champion skier	• Write an essay about someone you admire • Brainstorm, then plan an essay • Explain purpose and intention • Avoid errors with *so that*	*It's just the opposite!* • When you learn a new adjective or descriptive expression, find out how to express the opposite meaning	• *well* + adjective • Adverb and adjective collocations • Patterns with comparatives *pages 166–167*

Checkpoint 4 Units 10–12   pages 136–137

Getting along

In Unit 7, you . . .

- talk about getting along with people.
- use phrasal verbs.
- use infinitives and *-ing* forms.
- learn how to make your point clear.
- use *I have to say* to make a strong point.

Lesson A *House rules*

1 Vocabulary in context

A ◀)) CD 3.02 **What are house rules? Why do people have them? Think of one rule. Then read the article. Is your rule mentioned?**

Living with roommates

▶ You're **looking forward to** living with a roommate, but will you get along? Before you move in together, **come up with** some house rules about what you both expect. For example:

- If you **have** friends **over** for dinner, ask if it's OK *before* they show up.
- If you get back late, come in quietly – don't **wake** anyone **up**.
- If you're the last one to go to bed, turn off the TV and lights.
- If you borrow something, ask first and *always* **give** it **back**.

▶ Roommates often argue about chores. Instead of **putting up with** your roommate's mess, figure out some rules that work for you, like these:

- If you make a mess, **clean** it **up**.
- If you drop it, pick it up.
- If you take it out, put it back.

▶ If your roommate's bad habits still drive you crazy and you **run out of** patience, don't **put off** talking about it. When a problem **comes up, go over** things right away. Of course you might find out that you have to **give up** a few bad habits of your own! But with a little good humor, you'll get over any problems and things should work out.

About you

B **Pair work** **Complete the expressions in the questions with words from the article. Then take turns asking and answering the questions.**

Do you . . .

1. often **have** friends _____ ?
2. keep **running** _____ **of** cash?
3. ever **wake** anyone _____ ?
4. **put** _____ doing chores?
5. **go** _____ your bills?
6. always **give** things _____ ?
7. stay calm if a problem **comes** _____ ?
8. **come** _____ **with** ideas for meals?
9. have to **put** _____ **with** noisy neighbors?
10. ever try to **give** _____ bad habits?
11. **look** _____ **to** family dinners?
12. always **clean** _____ your mess?

Word sort

C **Complete a chart like this with the ideas in Exercise B. Then compare charts with a new partner.**

I . . .	I don't . . .
often have friends over.	have to put up with noisy neighbors.

Vocabulary notebook

See page 83.

2 Grammar Using phrasal verbs

Figure it out

A How does the article express the ideas in bold? Rewrite the sentences. Then read the grammar chart.

1. If you **arrive home** late, come in quietly.
2. If you're the last to go to bed, **don't leave** the lights **on**.
3. If you borrow a book, **return** it.
4. Don't **tolerate** your roommate's mess.

Grammar extra
See page 156.

Phrasal verbs ⬇

Intransitive phrasal verbs have no object. *come in, come up, get back, show up, work out*	*If you **get back** late, **come in** quietly.*
Some transitive phrasal verbs are separable. *clean up, give back, give up, put off, turn on/off, wake up*	**Turn off** the TV. OR **Turn** the TV **off**. **Turn** it **off**. (NOT ~~Turn off it~~.)
Some transitive phrasal verbs have a fixed word order. *get through, get over, go over + sb / sthg; have sb over*	*You'll **get over** the problem / it.* *I often **have** friends **over**.*
Some phrasal verbs also take a <u>preposition</u>. *come up with, look forward to, put up with, run out of*	*If you **run out of** patience, **come up with** some rules.*

About you

B Write the words in parentheses in the correct place in the sentences. If there is more than one possible answer, write both answers. Then ask and answer the questions with a partner.

1. Are you looking to having your own place? (forward) Do you plan to move with anyone? (in)
2. Have you come any rules for your home? (up with) What are they?
3. Do you always clean any mess right away? (up)
4. What problems come in your home? (up) Do things usually work? (out)
5. Has a friend ever shown early or late and woken your family? (up, up)
6. If you had a problem with your neighbors, would you put it? (up with) Or would you have them and go things? (over, over)
7. Do you borrow things from neighbors if you run them? (out of) Do you give them right away? (back)

C Pair work Agree on the six best house rules to have. Use a phrasal verb in each rule.

"How about – if you want to listen to music at 3:00 a.m., please turn it down so you don't wake me up."

3 Listening and speaking My worst roommate

A Pair work Imagine you had a roommate who did the things in the chart. Which problems would be the worst?

	The problem with my roommate was that he/she . . .		He/She didn't . . .
1. Marc	☐ a. got up late every day.	☐ b. used my things without asking.	
2. Hana	☐ a. didn't share the chores.	☐ b. had friends over all the time.	
3. Emilio	☐ a. woke me up early.	☐ b. didn't put things away.	
4. Cassie	☐ a. never cleaned up.	☐ b. always turned off my music.	

B ◀))CD 3.03 Listen to four people talk about roommates. What was each person's problem? Check (✔) a or b. Then listen again and write one thing each roommate didn't do.

About you

C Group work Agree on a way to solve each problem. Share your ideas with the class.

Lesson B *Does family size matter?*

1 Grammar in context

A CD 3.04 **Listen. Who is from a big family? Who is from a small family? Which two people were "only children"? Can you figure it out? Then read and check.**

"Only children" and siblings compare experiences growing up.

1 OSMAN

People often say, "It must be stressful to live like that." But it wasn't. There was always somebody to play with and share secrets with and everything. I think it's important for kids to be around other kids. I guess the only thing was, I used to long for somewhere quiet to study.

3 LILLI

Looking back, I don't know how my mom did it as a single parent. It was impossible for her to have time for herself. Still, we always had enough to eat, nice clothes to wear, books to read, etc. We were very close, maybe because it was just the three of us.

2 SOPHIA

I suppose I was a bit lonely being by myself all the time – I was always having to find ways to occupy myself. And like, there was no one else to blame if I got into trouble – I couldn't get away with anything! It's hard to tell how it affected me, but . . . it's not worth worrying about now, though.

4 SEAN

Personally, I had no real problems growing up. I got lots of attention, but I guess there was a lot of pressure on me to do well in school. I mean, I don't feel I missed out on anything. I had lots of opportunities to socialize with other kids in school.

B **Check (✔) the columns to give your personal answers to the questions.**
Then compare with a partner. Give reasons for your views.

Which of the people above do you think . . .	Osman	Sophia	Lilli	Sean	None
had a very happy childhood?					
had an unhappy childhood?					
missed having siblings (= brothers and sisters)?					
sometimes found family life stressful?					
enjoyed being with their siblings?					

2 Grammar Describing experiences

Figure it out

A Circle the correct verb forms to complete the sentences. Use the article to help you. Then read the grammar chart.

1. Osman thinks it's important for children **to grow up** / **growing up** with other children.
2. Sophia says that she was sometimes a little lonely **to play** / **playing** by herself.
3. Lilli says she always had enough **to eat** / **eating** as a child.
4. Sean feels that he had no real problems **to be** / **being** an only child.

Infinitives (*to* + verb) 🔽	-*ing* forms (verb + -*ing*)
After adjectives, you can use infinitives, especially in *It* clauses. This is common in generalizations. *It was* **impossible** *for her* **to have** *time for herself.*	You can also use -*ing* forms. This is common when people describe an actual experience. *I was a bit* **lonely being** *by myself all the time.*
After nouns or pronouns, use infinitives to add more details or say how you use them. *We always had nice* **clothes to wear**. *There was always* **someone to play with**.	After these expressions, use -*ing* forms: *have fun, have (no) trouble / problem(s); be worth.* *I* **had fun / no problems growing up** *in my family.* *It's not* **worth worrying** *about.*

Grammar extra See page 157.

Common errors

Don't add *for* or use *for* instead of *to*.
We had **books to read**. (NOT ~~for to read, for read~~)

In conversation . . .

After adjectives, infinitives are far more common.

About you

B Complete the comments with a correct form of the verbs. Sometimes there is more than one answer. Then discuss the views with a partner. Do you agree with each other?

1. It's hard _____ (imagine) growing up as an only child. I had six sisters, and we had lots of fun _____ (make up) games together. The advantage of a big family is that it's impossible _____ (be) lonely.
2. One disadvantage of being an only child is that I never had anybody _____ (share) problems with. I had no trouble _____ (find) kids _____ (play) with, though. I guess it makes you more independent.
3. I was the oldest, so it was my job _____ (take care of) my brothers. There were a lot of things _____ (do). Big families are OK, but parents don't have much time _____ (spend) with each kid.
4. My sister and I fought all the time. It was hard _____ (sit) in the same room without arguing. After she left home, it was easier _____ (be) together. Families don't always get along.

3 Viewpoint A big or small family?

A **Pair work** Is it better to grow up in a small family or in a big family? Discuss the advantages and disadvantages of each situation, and agree on an answer.

"Basically, it's better to be in a small family because you get more time with your parents, you know, one-on-one."

B **Class activity** Present your argument for a big family or a small family to the class. Then take a class vote.

In conversation . . .

You can use *Basically, . . .* to give your main opinion.

Lesson C *What I mean is . . .*

 Conversation strategy Making your meaning clear

A Which of these things should parents expect their children to do? At what point in their lives? In high school? In college? After college?

contribute to household bills	do household chores	move out	pay rent
cook their own meals	do their own laundry	pay for food	observe the house rules

B 🔊 CD 3.05 **Listen. What is Franco's problem? What is Sarah's view?**

Sarah So how are things going, now that you've graduated?

Franco OK, but it was hard moving back in with my parents. I'm not saying we don't get along, but frankly there's a bit of friction. You know, they have all these rules.

Sarah Well, I have to say, it *is* their house. What I mean is, it's probably not easy for them, either.

Franco I know. I'm just saying it's hard to get used to. And they've even asked me to pay rent now.

Sarah Well, . . . you'd have to pay rent if you had your own place.

Franco I know. I don't mean that they should support me completely, but I could use some help till I get on my feet. In other words, I just wish they'd give me a break.

Sarah Well, you could always work more hours if you need to.

C **Notice** how Sarah and Franco make their meaning clear by adding to or repeating their ideas. They use expressions like these. Find examples in the conversation.

> *What I'm saying is, . . .*   *I'm (just) saying . . .*
> *What I mean is, . . .*   *I'm not saying . . .*
> *I mean, . . .*   *I don't mean . . .*
> *In other words, . . .*

About you

D **Match the comments. Write the letters a–f. Then discuss with a partner. Are any of the situations true for you?**

1. I can't wait to get my own place. __d__
2. You can save money when you live at home. ____
3. I guess you have to live by your parents' rules. ____
4. My mom says I have to move out when I get a job. ____
5. I've always had to do my own laundry and stuff. ____
6. If you don't pay rent at home, you should still contribute somehow. ____

a. I'm just saying I can take care of myself and do that kind of thing.
b. What I mean is, you could help redecorate a room or something.
c. I don't mean that you shouldn't contribute toward rent, though.
✔ d. I'm not saying living with my parents is bad. But it'll be fun fixing up my own apartment.
e. What I'm saying is, you're really a guest in their home.
f. In other words, she just wants me to be independent, which is fine.

2 Strategy plus *I have to say . . .*

CD 3.06 You can use *I have to say* to show that you want to make a strong statement, often to say something controversial.

> Well, **I have to say**, it *is* their house.

In conversation . . .

You can use these expressions to say what you really feel.

Honestly	███████████
I have to say	███████
(Quite) frankly	██████
To be honest (with you)	█████
To tell you the truth	████

A CD 3.07 **Listen. Write the expressions you hear. Then practice with a partner.**

1. *A* Do you think it's hard for adult children to live with their parents?

   B I _____ don't think it is. Some of my friends complain about their parents. But _____ I think they're lucky to have a free place to live.

2. *A* Is it reasonable for parents to ask their kids to pay rent to live at home?

   B I don't really know, _____ . I know some parents who pay all their kids' expenses, and _____ I think that's a bad idea.

3. *A* When do you think is the best time for kids to move out and be independent?

   B _____ , I think it depends. I suppose after they get their first real job. Though my sister's working, and _____ , she couldn't afford to move out right now.

About you

B **Pair work** **Take turns asking the questions above and giving your own answers. Use expressions like *Honestly* to make strong statements and to say how you feel.**

3 Listening and strategies "Boomerang" kids

A **Read the advice for parents. Do you know any parents who have done these things?**

How to deal with your "boomerang" kids

- ☐ Set up a work-for-rent arrangement. _____
- ☐ Refuse to lend money. _____
- ☐ Don't buy clothes or personal items. _____
- ☐ Remove the TV from his/her bedroom. _____
- ☐ Insist he/she has to apply for a job every day. _____
- ☐ Insist he/she has to be home by 11:00 p.m. _____
- ☐ Set a move-out date. _____
- ☐ Have a no friends / no parties rule. _____

B CD 3.08 **Listen to two parents talk about "boomerang" children. Check (✔) the rules in Exercise A that Karen advises Steve to set.**

C CD 3.09 **Listen again. Does Steve think he can set each rule that Karen advises? Write Yes or No next to each rule in Exercise A.**

About you

D **Group work** **Which advice in Exercise A do you think is reasonable? Which is not? Can you think of other rules parents should make?**

"To be honest, I think it's reasonable to set up a work-for-rent arrangement. What I mean is, . . ."

4 Speaking naturally Conversational expressions *See page 141.*

Lesson D *How <u>not</u> to get along!*

1 Reading

A **Prepare** What do satirical articles do? Check (✔) the boxes below. Do you enjoy reading satire? Explain what you like or don't like about it.

Satirical articles . . .

- ☐ make fun of people.
- ☐ give a balanced view of an issue.
- ☐ use humor to criticize people.
- ☐ exaggerate or say the opposite of what's true.
- ☐ show respect for people or organizations.
- ☐ joke about social or political trends.

B **Read for style** Read this satirical article. Which of the things in Exercise A does it do? Give examples.

How to lose friends

| THE CITY WEEKLY | **community voices**

Now That I've Driven All My Friends Away, *I Finally Have Time For Me!*

by Bradley Crouch

¹Who needs friends? You work hard all day, and then they expect you to give up your evenings to hang out with them at movies and restaurants. That's exhausting, as well as expensive. You can't even take weekends off because there are parties, nightclubs, bike rides, beach trips, and more. Some friends will even try to tag along on your vacation! With friends like these, you won't have a moment to yourself.

²Luckily, I've found ways to get people like this off my back. Just follow the five steps below, and you, too, will finally have time to do lots of important things, like playing online games for hours on end, heating up microwave dinners, and watching late-night TV infomercials alone in the dark.

³**Step 1: Don't get around to calling them back**.
Don't feel guilty about not returning friends' calls. Just think of it this way. If a telemarketer left you a message, would you call back? Of course not! They just waste your time. Well, in the same way, your friends probably just want you to waste your time listening to their tedious stories. Just put off making those calls, or better still, ignore them completely!

⁴**Step 2: If you must talk, make it painful**.
Despite your best efforts to shake them all off, you may still end up talking to a friend. If this happens, talk about yourself – constantly. Friends hate this! Focus on topics that are boring, gross, or both, such as what time you woke up or an embarrassing medical problem. Just make sure you don't ask your friends any questions about themselves!

⁵**Step 3: Don't show up on time**.
Let's say you followed Steps 1 and 2, but your friends still managed to come up with plans for you. Maybe you agreed to see a movie together. What I would do in a case like this is arrive 30 minutes after the movie starts. That way you annoy your friends, but you still get to see most of the film. Or simply let them down and don't show up at all.

⁶**Step 4: Always be short of cash**.
Never bring money when you're out with friends. Let them pay! That will make your time with them less painful. After all, it's fun spending other people's money, especially when you have no intention of paying them back.

⁷**Step 5: Sit back and do nothing**.
As a result of taking the steps above, you should notice a growing emptiness in your calendar, inbox, and life. Congratulations! Now you can sit back and enjoy your freedom. Just think. The next time everyone else is stuck at another backyard barbecue, on a ski trip, or on a night out, you'll be at home alone, staring at your cell phone, which will never ring.

⁸So, I hope this all made sense and that you now have time for yourself – for a change.

Reading tip
Writers often start with a question that sets the scene for the topic or problem they are going to address.

C Understanding reference Find the expressions in the article. What do the underlined words refer to? Do they refer to ideas that come before or after them in the article? Complete the chart.

Expression	Paragraph	Refers to	Before?	After?
1. hang out with <u>them</u>	1	your friends	✔	
2. <u>That's</u> exhausting	1			
3. people like <u>this</u>	2			
4. the five steps <u>below</u>	2			
5. important <u>things</u>	2			
6. think of it <u>this way</u>	3			
7. If <u>this</u> happens	4			
8. Friends hate <u>this</u>	4			
9. <u>That way</u> you	5			

About you

D React Pair work Discuss the questions.

- Did you find the article humorous? Which parts did you find most amusing?
- Does the article make any serious points? What is the main message of the article?
- Which step would be most effective in getting rid of your friends?
- Have you ever done any of the things in the article? What happened?

2 Focus on vocabulary Idiomatic expressions

A Find the expressions in bold in the article. Figure out their meanings. Then match the two parts of the sentences to check your answers. Write the letters a–f.

1. If you **drive** your friends **away**, _____
2. If you **tag along** with someone, _____
3. If you **get** someone **off your back**, _____
4. If you don't **get around to** something, _____
5. If you **let** people **down**, _____
6. If you are **short of** or **on** something, _____

a. you don't find the time to do it.
b. you stop that person from annoying you.
c. you don't have enough of it.
d. you disappoint them.
e. you do things so they won't be your friends.
f. you go along even if you're not needed or invited.

B Pair work Take turns using the expressions in Exercise A to give advice on friendships.

"If you don't want to drive away your friends, it's a good idea to listen to them and . . ."

3 Viewpoint Who needs friends like these?

Group work Do you have problems like these with people you know? What other problems do people have with their friends? Discuss suggestions for solving the problems.

He never shows up on time.

He keeps letting me down at the last minute!

She always tags along with us – even if we don't invite her.

She's always short of money when it's time to pay the bill.

He talks about himself all the time.

He never gets around to returning my calls.

In conversation . . .

You can use these expressions to suggest solutions.
You could always tell her . . .
You might want to . . .
It's a good idea to . . .

"If people are always showing up late, it's a good idea to meet them at a café. I started doing that with a friend of mine, and now I don't feel so bad waiting for him anymore."

Writing *Friends or family?*

In this lesson, you . . .
- use a thesis statement.
- use *What* clauses for key points.
- avoid errors with subjects.

Task **Write an introduction to an essay.**
The saying "Blood is thicker than water" suggests that family relationships are more important than friendships. Do you agree?

A **Brainstorm** Discuss the essay question above with a partner, and take notes. Do you agree with the saying? Give three reasons for your opinion.

B **Look at a model** Read the introduction to an essay below. Underline the thesis statement.

Thesis statements

A thesis statement in your introduction tells the reader the main point or argument you will make.

> The expression "Blood is thicker than water" suggests that our relationships with family members are closer than the relationships we have with our friends. It implies that friendships are less important. On the one hand, it is fair to say that our family is an important part of our lives. Family members often put up with our annoying habits or support us when problems come up. On the other hand, our friends are the people that we choose to be in our lives and that choose us to be in theirs. Families do not have this choice. What is more important than being part of a family, in my view, is having a strong network of friends.

C **Focus on language** Read the grammar chart. Then rewrite the sentences below as *What* clauses. There is sometimes more than one way to rewrite them.

What clauses in writing ⬇

You can use a *What* clause in a sentence to give the most important information in a paragraph. *What* clauses are often the subject of the verb *be*. Notice that the verb is singular.

ADJECTIVE	NOUN	TO + VERB		*THAT* CLAUSE

*What is **important** is **a network of friends**. / **to have** close friends. / **that you have** friends.*

VERB	NOUN	*TO* + VERB

*What we all **want** is **good friends**. / **to have** good friends.*

In writing . . .

You can write a thesis statement with other structures, but a *What* clause is a good choice.

VERB	*THAT* CLAUSE

*What this **implies** is **that you should respect your friends**.*

1. It's essential to have a good relationship with your family. _____
2. Everyone needs the support of their family. _____
3. It's important to show respect to your family members. _____
4. It's clear – family relationships are stronger than friendships. _____
5. This means that blood really is thicker than water. _____

D **Write and check** Look back at the Task at the top of the page. Write an introduction to an essay. Use a *What* clause in your thesis statement. Then check for errors.

Common errors

Sentences need a subject.

What is important *is to have good friends.*
It *is important to have good friends.*
(NOT *Is important . . .*)

Vocabulary notebook *Look forward to it!*

When you learn a new expression, such as a phrasal verb, use it in a true sentence about someone you know. Describe the person or your relationship with him or her. Write notes next to a photograph.

My sister is great. I always look forward to spending time with her.

A Write the names of people you know to make these sentences true.

1. _____ has never run out of money.
2. _____ puts off everything until the last minute.
3. I always look forward to seeing _____ .
4. _____ gave up a job one time.
5. I like to have _____ over for dinner.

We're running out of . . .

The things people talk about *running out* of most are:
time
money
space
breath

B Now write the name of someone you know in a photo frame. Add a photo if you can. How many of the phrasal verbs in the box can you use about the person?

clean up	come up with	give up	look forward to	run out of
come up	give back	go over	put up with	wake up

Magdi

We always go over our homework together.

_____

_____

_____

C Word builder Find the meanings of the phrasal verbs below. Can you use them to write about the person in Exercise B?

1. get around to (doing) something _____
2. come across (as) _____
3. go along with _____
4. go through _____
5. look out for someone _____
6. look up to someone _____

This is my mom, who puts up with me and my sister.

On your own

Make an online photo album of your friends and family. Write a caption for each photo, using a phrasal verb.

Food science

In Unit 8, you . . .

- talk about food, farming, and nutrition.
- use the passive to talk about the past, present, and future.
- use verb complements.
- use rhetorical questions to make a point.
- add examples as part of your argument.

Lesson A *Vertical farming*

 Grammar in context

A **What kinds of farms are there in your country? What do they grow or produce? Which foods does your country import and export?**

B ◀))CD 3.12 **Listen to the radio interview. Which photo best illustrates the topic?**

> **HOME**
> **LISTEN LIVE**
> **PROGRAMS**
> **8 PODCASTS**
>
> **Anchor** By the year 2025, the world population is expected to rise to 8 billion. In order to grow enough food, it is estimated that 1 billion hectares (almost 2.5 billion acres) of new land will be needed – that is, if the farming methods that are practiced today continue. Environmentalists say something must be done if food shortages are going to be avoided. That's why the idea of "vertical farming" is being discussed at an eco-conference this week. Celia Hernandez, our environmental correspondent, joins me. Celia, what is vertical farming? And where did the idea come from?
>
> **Celia** The idea was developed by Dickson Despommier, a professor at Columbia University, back in 1999. Vertical farms are basically high-rise greenhouses that can be built in cities. So crops will be grown indoors – and in water, instead of in soil.
>
> **Anchor** And what are the advantages of growing food in this way?
>
> **Celia** Well, supporters say it's more reliable because crops won't be affected by weather conditions like drought or cold. It's also more environmentally friendly, because waste can be composted and water will be recycled. And because crops will be grown, harvested, and consumed in the same urban area, transportation costs will be greatly reduced. So in theory, food should be cheaper, too.

C Pair work **Answer the questions about the interview.**

- Why is vertical farming an important topic?
- What will vertical farms look like? Where will they be?
- In what ways are vertical farms different from conventional farms?
- Why will vertical farming probably make food cheaper?

2 Grammar Information focus

Figure it out

A How might the journalists say the sentences below? Rewrite the sentences, starting with the words given. Use the interview to help you. Then read the grammar chart.

1. Some people expect the population to rise by 3 billion. *The population . . .*
2. Dickson Despommier invented the idea. *The idea . . .*
3. The weather won't affect crops. *Crops . . .*

The passive

Grammar extra
See page 158.

You can use the passive to make the "receiver" of an action the focus, when you don't know the "doer," or if you feel the "doer" is not important. You can introduce the "doer" with *by*.

Active sentences	Passive sentences
Experts **expect** the population to rise.	The population **is expected** to rise.
A professor **developed** the idea.	The idea **was developed by** a professor.
They **haven't built** vertical farms.	Vertical farms **haven't been built**.
They**'re going to discuss** the issue.	The issue **is going to be discussed**.
They**'ll grow** crops in water.	Crops **will be grown** in water.
The weather **won't affect** crops.	Crops **won't be affected by** the weather.
Someone **must do** something.	Something **must be done**.

B ◀)) CD 3.13 Rewrite the underlined parts of the sentences from the rest of the interview. Use the passive and add *by* where it is needed. Then listen and check your answers.

crops will be grown

1. *A* So <u>they will grow crops</u> in water? I know <u>they do this</u> already, but how does it work?

   B Well, <u>they add nutrients</u> to the water. So <u>the plants use less energy</u> to get the nutrients. And plants that <u>they grow</u> in this way grow faster and bigger.

2. *A* People often say that <u>they use too many pesticides</u> in farming. Do vertical farms use them?

   B Um, no, <u>they won't need pesticides</u>. This is because <u>they'll protect the crops</u> inside the building. So <u>they will reduce the use of pesticides</u>. And groundwater, which <u>pesticides have contaminated</u> for years, will be cleaner.

3. *A* Now, reports say that <u>we are going to see vertical farms</u> in our cities soon. Is that true?

   B Well, <u>they can't build them</u> without more research. <u>They carried out some trials</u> last year and <u>they wrote a report</u>, but <u>they haven't published it</u> yet. I'd say <u>they're not going to build them</u> anytime soon. But environmentalists say <u>we must not ignore the situation and should take action</u> soon because <u>we're going to need more food</u> with the population increasing by 5,000 a day. They say that <u>we need to find a solution</u> soon.

C Group work Discuss the advantages and disadvantages of vertical farming.

A One of the biggest advantages is that food will be grown and sold in the same area.
B So transportation costs will be reduced and foods won't need to be packaged.
C Yes, but the only thing is that jobs will be lost and . . .

Lesson B *Food for health*

① Vocabulary in context

A CD 3.14 **How many foods can you think of that are good for your health? Make a list. Read the website article below. Which of your foods are mentioned?**

Top foods for health . . .

Don't let your diet make you unhealthy. The right foods can help you stay fit, boost your energy levels, and make you feel great.

10. Both kiwis and mangoes are said to keep your **eyesight** from deteriorating.

9. You may know that milk helps strengthen **bones** and **teeth**, but did you know that soybeans and tofu do, too?

8. Snack on pineapple. It benefits the **digestive system** and might keep you from getting an upset stomach.

7. Apples are thought to help to remove toxins from your **liver**. Raisins can help you build strong **muscles**.

6. In studies in South Korea, chili peppers have been shown to increase your **metabolism**, which may contribute to weight loss.

1. Blueberries are said to be good for your **brain**. They can help you concentrate and improve your memory. Have a headache? Try cherries to make the pain go away.

2. Use ginger in your cooking. It's thought to reduce cholesterol, which may protect you from getting **heart** disease.

3. Eating too much salt may cause your **blood pressure** to rise. But did you know that hibiscus tea is believed to lower it?

4. Avocados are good for your **skin**. But don't just eat them! Applying avocado to your skin may prevent it from aging.

5. Mushrooms are said to boost your **immune system**, which can protect you from getting colds or the flu.

Word sort

B **Make a chart like this with words from the website.**

Food	What it may be good for	The benefit
blueberries cherries	your brain headaches	can help you concentrate make pain go away

Vocabulary notebook

See page 93.

2 Grammar Describing causes and results

Figure it out

A Circle the correct option in each question. Use the article to help you. Then read the grammar chart.

1. Which fruits are said to help you **keep** / **keeping** your eyesight in good condition?
2. What might cause your blood pressure **rise** / **to rise** if you have too much of it?
3. What might mushrooms prevent you **from getting** / **to get**?

Grammar extra
See page 159.

Verb complements ⬇

Verb + object + verb
help*, let, make
*Can also be used with an infinitive.

Blueberries are said to **help** you **concentrate**.
Make the pain **go away** with cherries.

Verb + object + infinitive
allow, cause, enable, help

Eating too much salt may **cause** your blood pressure **to rise**.
Researchers say chili peppers **enable** you **to lose** weight.

Verb + object + from + -ing form
keep, prevent*, protect, stop*
*Can also be used without from.

Avocado may **prevent** / **stop** your skin **(from) aging**.
Kiwis are said to **keep** your eyesight **from deteriorating**.

In conversation . . .
The pattern help + object + verb is more common than help + object + infinitive.

B Complete the sentences with a correct form of the verbs given. Add *from* if necessary. Sometimes there is more than one answer.

1. The sugar in soda can cause your blood pressure _____ (rise). Fruits like watermelon and tomatoes are said to help you _____ (lower) it.
2. Don't let dinner with friends _____ (make) you heavier. Research shows that eating with friends makes you _____ (eat) up to 33 percent more food.
3. Asparagus may stop you _____ (have) mood swings. It's thought to help some people _____ (cope) with depression.
4. Chocolate may enable you _____ (concentrate) better. Some studies have also found that it protects your skin _____ (age).
5. Some studies seem to show that green tea contains chemicals which may prevent you _____ (get) certain types of cancer.
6. People who allow themselves _____ (eat) treats occasionally generally stay thinner.
7. If kids don't eat breakfast regularly, it may keep them _____ (perform) well on tests. However, too many sugary breakfast foods may make kids _____ (behave) badly.
8. One possible way to keep your skin _____ (get) dry is to drink lots of water!

About you

C Pair work Which of the ideas in Exercise B did you know about? Which ideas will make you change your eating habits? How?

"I didn't know the sugar in soda makes your blood pressure rise. That might make me drink less."

3 Viewpoint Top tips for eating well

Pair work Decide on your top ten tips for eating well to put on a health website. Then share ideas with another pair.

A OK. How about, "Drink water. It stops your skin from getting dry."
B All right. And we could add, "It may prevent your skin from aging."

In conversation . . .
You can use *All right* and *OK* to start a new topic or to agree.

Lesson C *Why do they do that?*

 Conversation strategy Using questions to make a point

A Read the three research findings. Are you like these average consumers?

- Only 50 percent of young adult consumers read the ingredients on food labels.
- U.S. consumers spend about 90 percent of their food budget on processed foods that contain additives like food coloring and artificial flavors.
- Many people believe the marketing claims that manufacturers make, even though some of them may be misleading.

B ◀)) CD 3.15 Listen. What's the problem with food, according to Edward and Debra?

Edward I think the main problem with our diet these days is that we eat too much processed food. Take cereal, for instance. If you look at the list of ingredients, you can't even pronounce most of them.

Debra Oh, I know.

Edward I mean, can all those additives be good for you?

Debra Yeah, and look at food coloring and artificial flavors. I mean, why do they need to add that stuff?

Edward I know. I imagine most people don't read the labels.

Debra And then the manufacturers make all those claims such as "Lowers your cholesterol." I mean, do most people really believe that stuff? I think a lot of those claims are misleading.

Edward Yeah, I have to say, we're not very well-informed about food, generally.

C **Notice** how Edward and Debra use rhetorical questions to make their point. They don't expect each other to answer these questions. Find two more examples in the conversation.

> *. . . can all those additives be good for you?*

D ◀)) CD 3.16 Complete the rest of Edward and Debra's conversation with the rhetorical questions in the box. Listen and check. Then practice the whole conversation.

Debra Yeah, I guess. My parents taught me about food when I was growing up. _____ It's so important.

Edward It is. But part of the problem is that healthy food costs so much more. I mean, _____

Debra And the trouble is, most people have forgotten how to prepare food properly. _____ Everyone just lives on fast food.

Edward I know. I think we've just forgotten what real food is.

a. why is it so expensive?

b. Isn't it a shame?

c. Why don't people cook anymore?

d. Why don't they educate kids about these issues?

_____

About you | **E** **Pair work** Discuss the points that Edward and Debra make. Which points do you agree or disagree with? Use rhetorical questions to make your point.

2 Strategy plus Giving examples

CD 3.17 You can use these expressions to give examples.

They make claims **such as / like** "Lowers your cholesterol."
Some claims are misleading – **for instance, / for example,** "low fat."
Take cereal, **for instance**.
Look at food coloring.

Take cereal, for instance.

About you

Complete the sentences with your own ideas. Then compare with your group. How many different ideas did you think of?

1. A lot of fast foods make you gain weight. Take _____ , for instance. They're full of fat.
2. Snack foods often have too much salt in them. Look at _____ , for example.
3. Manufacturers make a lot of claims on food packages. I've seen claims like _____ , for example.
4. They say the healthiest foods are fresh fruits and vegetables. Things such as _____ and _____ .
5. Lots of things are added to processed food, you know, things like _____ .

3 Listening and strategies A food revolution!

A **Look at the photos of Jamie Oliver, a famous British chef. What do you think he's doing in each picture? Discuss with a partner.**

B **CD 3.18** **Listen to two radio show hosts talk about Jamie Oliver. Number the photos in Exercise A in the correct order 1–5.**

C **CD 3.19** **Listen again. Answer the questions. Then compare with a partner.**

1. Why did Jamie Oliver start a TV series in the United States?
2. Why did Jamie start a petition?
3. What did the school chefs think about him at first?
4. What kind of impact has Jamie had?

About you

D **CD 3.20** **Pair work** **Listen to five people talk about Jamie Oliver. Discuss each reaction. Give your views and use rhetorical questions to make your point.**

A I agree. I mean, who has time to cook without using some processed foods? And some are probably fine.
B Yeah, take frozen vegetables. They're processed and they're OK.

4 Speaking naturally Strong and weak prepositions *See page 141.*

Lesson D *Where did all the bees go?*

1 Reading

A Prepare What do you know about bees? How many facts can you think of?

Bees live in hives.

B ⬇ Read for main ideas Read the article. What problem does the article describe? Why is it serious? What are the possible causes?

Where did all the bees go?

[1] The majority of people probably don't pay much attention to bees, except perhaps on the rare occasion that they're stung by one. However, that all changed with the publication of numerous articles several years ago, which reported a strange phenomenon called "colony-collapse disorder" (CCD). Beekeepers had been opening their hives, only to discover that many of their bees had mysteriously disappeared – and suddenly beekeeping became a hot news topic.

[2] According to the reports, some beekeepers had lost more than 70 percent of their bee colonies, and commercial beekeepers even reported losses of up to 90 percent. It was an alarming discovery, considering that bees pollinate over 90 of America's flowering crops – including avocados, cucumbers, and soybeans – as well as a range of fruit crops from apples to cranberries and kiwis.

[3] "This is the biggest general threat to our food supply," said agricultural scientist Kevin Hackett. He has a point. According to the U.S. Department of Agriculture, approximately one-third of our diet comes from plants that are pollinated by insects, and the honeybee is responsible for about 80 percent of that pollination. A Cornell University study estimated that bees pollinate more than $14 billion worth of U.S. seeds and crops annually.

[4] One example is the lucrative billion-dollar U.S. almond crop, which accounts for over 70 percent of the world's commercial production of almonds, and which is entirely dependent on honeybees. It is estimated that the almond crop alone would need about 1.5 million hives – roughly two-thirds of the colonies in the U.S. – to produce a successful harvest.

[5] U.S. farmers were not the only ones facing this problem. A similar decline in the bee population was reported in Canada, Brazil, and parts of Europe. Researchers worldwide started looking for answers, and a range of theories for the losses soon emerged. One theory was that the bees were dying from a virus, a parasite, or a fungus infection. Other theories blamed poor bee nutrition, pesticides, and cell phone radiation. It was also suggested that bees are simply stressed, because they are now raised to survive a shorter off-season and work more intensively than ever before.

[6] Since the total number of beehives has dropped by a quarter and the number of beekeepers has fallen by half, demand for beekeeping services has pushed up farmers' costs. The cost of renting a hive rose from $55 to $135 in three years. Many more beekeepers now travel across the country with their colonies, trucking some tens of billions of bees with them to pollinate crops. Others have started importing bees to keep up with demand. None of these solutions, however, really addresses the underlying problem. A solution needs to be found because without bees our food supply is threatened and our very survival is at stake. So the critical question remains not only, "What caused the disappearance of the bees?" but "What can we do about this terrible loss?"

C Understanding statistics Are the statistics true (T) or false (F)? Write T or F. Correct the false statistics.

1. Some beekeepers lost more than 70 percent of their bee colonies. _____
2. For others, only about 10 percent of their bees survived. _____
3. Bees pollinate all the flowering crops in the United States. _____
4. Two-thirds of what we eat comes from plants that are pollinated by insects. _____
5. Bees pollinate up to $14 billion worth of U.S. seeds and crops each year. _____
6. The United States grows less than half of the world's almonds. _____
7. It would take exactly two-thirds of the bees in the U.S. to pollinate the almond crop. _____
8. There are 50 percent fewer beekeepers now. _____

About you **D** Pair work Discuss the information in Exercise C. Which facts did you find surprising?

2 Focus on vocabulary Nouns and verbs

A Complete the questions with the noun forms of the verbs given. Use the article to help you. The paragraph numbers are in parentheses.

1. Who made the _____ (discover) that bees were disappearing? How? (para. 2)
2. Why is _____ (pollinate) so important? (para. 3)
3. What _____ (threaten) does colony-collapse disorder pose? (para. 3)
4. How important are honeybees in the _____ (produce) of almonds? (para. 4)
5. What theories are there to explain the _____ (disappear) of so many bees? (para. 6)
6. Do you think our _____ (survive) is really at stake? (para. 6)
7. How would the _____ (lose) of the bee population affect your life, do you think? (para. 6)

B Pair work Ask and answer the questions in Exercise A. Refer back to the article on page 90 to support your answers.

3 Listening and speaking Backyard beekeeping

A ◀)) CD 3.23 Listen to a radio interview with a beekeeper. Check (✔) the topics he talks about.

☐ How he became interested in bees ☐ How to care for a hive
☐ How bees actually pollinate flowers ☐ The dangers of beekeeping

B ◀)) CD 3.24 Listen to more of the interview, and complete the statistics.

1. A hive can produce about _____ pounds of honey a week.
2. Bees visit something like _____ flowers to produce a pound of honey.
3. The beekeeper has over _____ bees.
4. There are roughly _____ bees in a hive.
5. Bees travel up to _____ miles to pollinate crops.

C ◀)) CD 3.25 Listen to the last part of the interview. Write two advantages and two disadvantages of backyard beekeeping.

About you **D** Pair work Discuss the advantages and disadvantages of beekeeping. Would you ever keep bees? Why? Why not?

"I think backyard beekeeping is a good idea for several reasons. Firstly, it can help . . ."

You know what they say... busy as bees!

HONEY

DONNELLY

Writing *Ups and downs*

In this lesson, you . . .
- write about graphs, charts, and trends.
- use prepositions and approximate numbers.
- avoid errors with *fall, rise* and *grow*.

Task Write a report for a science class.

What's happening to bees?

A Look at a model Match each graph or chart with two sentences below. Write the letters a–d next to the sentences.

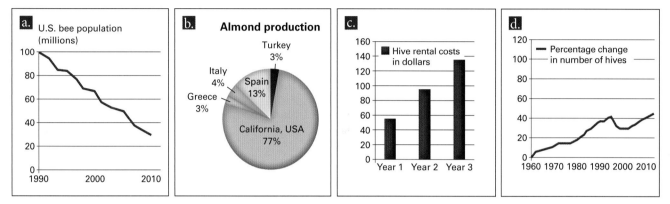

1. The cost of renting a hive rose from $55 to $135 in three years. __c__
2. There was a decline in the U.S. bee population of approximately 70 percent. _____
3. The majority of almonds are grown in the United States. _____
4. The number of bee colonies in the U.S. fell by more than 70 percent. _____
5. There was an increase in the number of hives worldwide of about 45 percent. _____
6. The U.S. accounted for over 70 percent of global almond production. _____
7. Globally, the number of hives increased by roughly 45 percent. _____
8. There was a rise of just over 145 percent in the cost of hives. _____

B Focus on language Read the grammar chart. Then circle the correct preposition, and add an appropriate expression to give an approximate number in the news report below.

Prepositions in writing ⬇	Approximate numbers		
The bee population ***declined by*** more than 70%.	**+/–**	about / approximately / roughly	
Globally, the number of hives ***increased by*** about 45%.	**+**	over / more than	
There was a ***decline in*** the bee population ***of*** over 70%.	**–**	under / less than	
A ***rise of*** 145% ***in*** the cost of hives affected farmers.	**>|**	nearly / almost / up to	

Researchers are concerned about the decline **in / by** bee colonies. Some blame hard winters. In a normal winter, the number of bees in a hive drops **by / for** _____ (+/–) 10 percent. However, in recent years, beekeepers have seen an annual fall **in / of** _____ (+/–) 30 percent **in / of** the number of bees in their hives. Some had losses **by / of** _____ (+/–) 50 percent, and some even lost _____ (>\|) 90 percent of their bees. Overall, the U.S. experienced a decline **of / in** _____ (+) 70% **in / by** its total bee population. However, this problem does not exist everywhere. In fact, globally, there has been an increase **by / of** _____ (+) 45 percent **from / in** _____ the number of hives, and honey production has also risen **by / in** _____ (+/–) 100 percent in the last 50 years.

C Write and check Look at the Task at the top of the page. Write your report. Then check for errors.

Common errors

Don't add *down* and *up* to the verbs *fall, rise,* and *grow* to describe trends.
*The bee population **fell,** then **rose/grew**.*
(NOT . . . ~~fell down / rose up / grew up~~)

Vocabulary notebook *Picture this!*

a heart   a heart

A   Label the pictures below with the words in the box. Then write health tips for each picture.

blood pressure	digestive system	eyesight	✓ immune system	teeth

1.

immune system

Mushrooms boost your immune system.

2.

_____

_____

3.

_____

_____

4.

_____

_____

5.

_____

_____

> **On the other hand . . .**
>
> *Hand* is the body part that is used the most in expressions in conversation. The most common are:
> *on the one hand*
> *on the other hand*
> *(get) out of hand*
> *(do something) by hand*

B   Now create a document on your computer for these words. Use an Internet search engine, and find pictures for each one. Write a health tip for each picture.

1. skin	2. bones	3. muscles	4. brain	5. liver

C   Word builder Find the meanings of the words in the box. Then find and label pictures like the one above.

circulation	joints	kidneys	lungs	sinuses

Eat blueberries – they're good for your brain.

On your own

Make a food chart for your kitchen wall. Use pictures from magazines and add health tips. See how many of the items you can eat or drink in one week!

Success and happiness

In Unit 9, you . . .

- talk about success and happiness.
- use *all, both, each, every, neither, none of, no.*
- learn more uses of *-ing* forms.
- use expressions like *in terms of* to focus in on your ideas.
- give opinions with expressions like *As far as I'm concerned, . . .*

↑ Success

↗ Opportunity

Lesson A *Successful people*

① Vocabulary in context

A ◀)) CD 3.26 **Make a list of well-known successful people. What makes them successful? Then read the article. Do the people on your list have the qualities described in the article?**

Three characteristics of successful people

1. Vision All successful people know they won't **get anywhere** without a vision. Fred Smith's vision was for an overnight package-delivery company. One of his college professors reportedly didn't think the idea would **get off the ground.** Nevertheless, Fred pursued his vision, and today FedEx is one of the world's largest delivery companies.

Mark Zuckerberg

Mark Zuckerberg had a vision for a social networking website and dropped out of college to **get** it **under way.** How Facebook **got to be** one of the most widely used networking sites is considered a marketing phenomenon. Both men became billionaires.

2. Persistence No success comes easily. Akio Morita, founder of Sony, sold fewer than 100 of his first rice cookers. Harland Sanders's Kentucky Fried Chicken recipe was rejected

1,009 times before a restaurant accepted it. Neither product **got off to a good start**, but neither of the entrepreneurs let failure **get them down** or **get in their way**. In fact, it's rare to find successful people who *haven't* experienced any setbacks. However, they tend to learn from their failures and **get on with** the job of rebuilding their businesses.

3. Passion Every successful person **gets ahead** in life because they simply love what they do. Celebrity chef Rachael Ray had no formal training in culinary arts, but loved creating recipes and built a career around it. In fact, history is full of people who **got to the top** by doing things they loved – Andre Agassi, Ralph Lauren, Sir Richard Branson. Each one was successful, and none of them graduated from college.

Rachael Ray

About you

B **Pair work** **Find expressions in the article to replace the words in bold below. Do you agree with the sentences? Discuss with a partner.**

1. You won't **succeed** in life or **go as far as you can** in your career if you don't like what you do.
2. It's not hard to **start** a business, but only businesses that **start out well** will be successful.
3. You won't **make any progress** in life if you don't have a passion.
4. Failure only **becomes** a problem if you let it **make you unhappy.**
5. Successful people don't let anything **stop them.** They **continue** building their businesses.

Word sort

C **Complete the chart with *get* expressions from the article.**

starting things	problems	making progress
		(not) get anywhere

Vocabulary notebook

See page 103.

② Grammar Talking about *all* and *none*

Figure it out

A Rewrite the sentences below, replacing the underlined words with phrases from the article. Then read the grammar chart.

1. Every successful person knows you need a vision.
2. The two men became billionaires.
3. The two products didn't sell at first.
4. Not one of these people graduated from college.
5. Success doesn't come easily.

Determiners 🔽		*Grammar extra* *See page 160.*
Singular nouns	**Each** entrepreneur was successful. **Every** restaurant rejected the recipe.	**No** entrepreneur wants to fail. **No** restaurant accepted the recipe.
Both (= two)	**Both** products got off to a good start. **Both (of)** these men became billionaires.	**Neither** product was a success at first. **Neither of** the men let failure get them down.
Plural nouns	**All** successful people have a vision. **All (of)** these people were successful.	**No** successful people get ahead easily. **None of** these people graduated from college.
Uncountable nouns	**All (of)** their hard work paid off.	**None of** their hard work was wasted.

About you

B Circle the correct determiners in the conversations. Then practice with a partner. Practice again, this time giving your own answers and ideas.

1. *A* Do you know any successful people?
   B Yes. **Each / All** my close friends are successful. They worked hard, and **all of / every** their efforts paid off. **None / No** success is easy. **None of / No** my friends had it easy, anyhow.

2. *A* In what way are the people you know successful?
   B Well, **both / each** person is successful in a different way. One's happily married with kids. One's a nurse. Another's very wealthy. But **all of / every** friend I have is doing what they love.

3. *A* What do you think successful people have in common?
   B Well, they take risks. Two businesspeople I know got off to a bad start, but **neither of / neither** their companies failed in the end. They didn't let fear of failure get in their way.

4. *A* What successes have you had in life so far? How did they make you feel?
   B Well, I graduated from college. I'm sure **every / all** student is happy to graduate, but for me college wasn't easy. **Each / Both of** my roommates thought I would quit.

③ Viewpoint The five laws of success

A 🔊 CD 3.27 **Listen. Take notes on what each person says is most important about success.**

B Pair work **Now discuss the ideas. Do you agree? Decide on your top five laws of success, and share them with another pair.**

A It seems to me that every successful person has a positive outlook.
B Absolutely. You can get anywhere in life with a positive outlook.

> **In conversation . . .**
> You can say *It seems to me* to give an opinion.

So which IS the right way?

THE ROAD TO SUCCESS

DONNELLY

Lesson B *Happy moments*

Grammar in context

A **What are some of the happiest moments in life? Share your ideas as a class.**

"Well, one of the happiest moments in life is when you graduate from college."

B ◀))CD 3.28 **Listen. What were some of the happiest moments in Anna's and Wesley's lives? Practice the conversation.**

Anna I think some of the happiest moments in my life were playing on this beach as a kid.

Wesley Yeah? My happiest moment was graduating from college, when all that hard work finally paid off.

Anna You know, college really wasn't my thing. I mean, I tried to make the most of it. But I got so stressed, taking exams all the time. I remember sitting outside on the last night, talking. My friends were out there with me, crying. And I was sitting there, thinking, "Gosh, I'm glad it's all over!"

Wesley And look at you now – with a successful career and everything.

Anna I know. There are so many things going on in my life. And being successful feels good. But it's not everything. Remember when we were kids and we'd run around, playing in the sand, not caring about anything?

Wesley Yeah. Hey, look – there are some people digging for clams over there. Want to look for some?

Anna Sure. Come on. I'll race you!

C **Pair work** **Discuss the questions. Do you share the same interpretation?**

1. What do you think Anna and Wesley's relationship is?
2. Who do you think is more successful? Why?
3. Who do you think sounds happier? Why?

About you

D **Pair work** **Find the expressions in bold in the conversation and check their meaning. Then ask and answer the questions.**

1. Do you think hard work always **pays off**?
2. Have you ever done anything that wasn't **your thing**?
3. Are you **making the most** of your classes?
4. Will you be glad when your studies are **all over**?
5. What good things **are going on** in your life?
6. Do you believe that success **isn't everything**?

"I think hard work always pays off. You won't get anywhere if you're lazy."

2 **Grammar** Adding information

A **How do Anna and Wesley say these things? Find the sentences. Then read the grammar chart.**

1. There are so many things that are going on.
2. I got so stressed when I took exams.
3. My happiest moment was when I graduated.
4. When you're successful, it feels good.

-ing forms	Grammar extra See page 161.
An -ing form can be a reduced relative clause.	There are some people **digging** for clams. I've got so many things **going on** in my life.
An -ing form can describe one event that happens at the same time as another. Notice the commas.	We'd run around, **playing** in the sand, **not caring** . . . I was sitting there, **thinking**.
An -ing form can come before or after be. It can be the subject or object of a verb.	My happiest moments were **playing** on this beach. **Being** successful is/feels good. I remember **sitting** outside.

B ◀))CD 3.29 **Rewrite the anecdotes so that each sentence uses an -ing form from the grammar chart. You will need to cross out words, change verbs, or do both. Then listen and check.**

having

1. **One of the happiest moments in my life was** ~~when I had~~ dinner in Italy with my husband. We were on a little island on a lake, and we were eating outside at a restaurant. And there were these musicians who were playing music. The moment when we watched the sunset was so romantic. I can't remember when I felt happier.

2. **I think the happiest day in my life was** the day I celebrated my 18th birthday and played volleyball on the beach. There were some other guys there who were playing a game, too, and we played against them. They were really good, so the fact that we won felt really great. We've all stayed friends ever since, and when we get together, it always reminds me of that day.

3. **My earliest happy memory was** when I won the school spelling bee. I felt so proud as I stood there. Everyone in the audience stood up and clapped. And when I saw my parents' faces, it was the best moment. I stood on the stage for ages and didn't want it all to end.

C **Pair work** **Talk about happy moments in your life. Use the words in bold in Exercise B to start.**

3 **Listening and speaking** Happy moments gone wrong!

A ◀))CD 3.30 **Listen to three people talk about moments that went wrong. Number the topics 1–3. There are three extra topics.**

_____ a graduation ceremony   _____ a birthday   _____ moving into a new home
_____ opening night at a play   _____ a marriage proposal   _____ a dream vacation

B ◀))CD 3.31 **Listen again. Answer the questions in the chart for each person.**

	What went wrong?	How did each person feel?	
1. José		☐ a. annoyed	☐ b. worried
2. Cho Hee		☐ a. angry	☐ b. embarrassed
3. Katy		☐ a. disappointed	☐ b. confused

C **Group work** **Discuss the situations in Exercises A and B. How would you have felt? Tell your group any stories you know about when things went wrong.**

Lesson C *As far as happiness goes, . . .*

 1 Conversation strategy Focusing in on a topic

A Do you agree with this statement? Why or why not?

"The best way to define happiness is in terms of success."

B 🔊 CD 3.32 **Listen to a group discussion in a psychology class. Which comments do you agree with?**

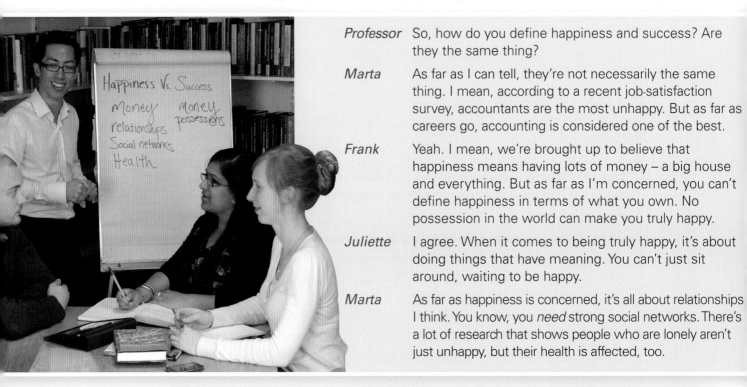

Professor	So, how do you define happiness and success? Are they the same thing?
Marta	As far as I can tell, they're not necessarily the same thing. I mean, according to a recent job-satisfaction survey, accountants are the most unhappy. But as far as careers go, accounting is considered one of the best.
Frank	Yeah. I mean, we're brought up to believe that happiness means having lots of money – a big house and everything. But as far as I'm concerned, you can't define happiness in terms of what you own. No possession in the world can make you truly happy.
Juliette	I agree. When it comes to being truly happy, it's about doing things that have meaning. You can't just sit around, waiting to be happy.
Marta	As far as happiness is concerned, it's all about relationships I think. You know, you *need* strong social networks. There's a lot of research that shows people who are lonely aren't just unhappy, but their health is affected, too.

C **Notice** how the students use expressions like these to focus in on a topic. Find the examples in the conversation.

> **As far as (success) is concerned, . . .**
> **As far as (careers) go, . . .**
> **When it comes to happiness / being happy, . . .**
> **. . . in terms of . . .**

In conversation . . .

These expressions are more common in formal speaking.

	Conversation	Formal speaking
in terms of	▪	▪▪▪▪▪▪
As far as . . . concerned	▪	▪▪▪
When it comes to	▪	▪▪

About you

D **Complete the sentences with your own ideas. Then compare with a partner.**

1. When it comes to being truly happy, _____ is/are more important than _____ .

2. As far as true happiness is concerned, it has nothing to do with _____ .

3. As far as having a successful career goes, you _____ .

4. You can't define success just in terms of _____ .

5. As far as relationships are concerned, it's important _____ .

"When it comes to being truly happy, good relationships are more important than anything."

2 Strategy plus *As far as I . . .*

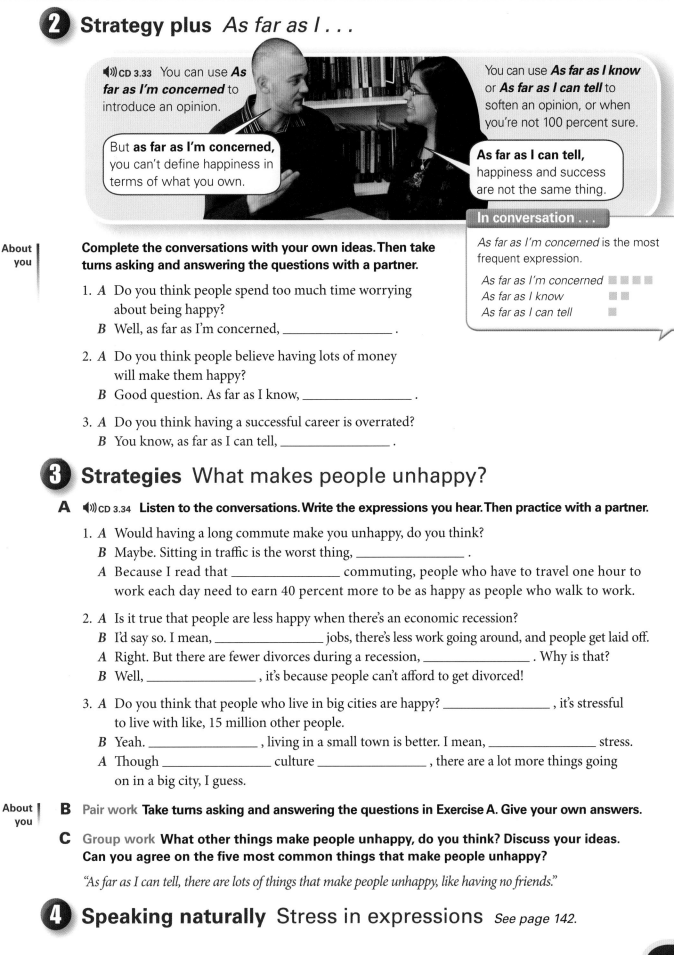

CD 3.33 You can use *As far as I'm concerned* to introduce an opinion.

But **as far as I'm concerned,** you can't define happiness in terms of what you own.

You can use *As far as I know* or *As far as I can tell* to soften an opinion, or when you're not 100 percent sure.

As far as I can tell, happiness and success are not the same thing.

In conversation . . .

As far as I'm concerned is the most frequent expression.

As far as I'm concerned	■ ■ ■ ■
As far as I know	■ ■
As far as I can tell	■

About you | **Complete the conversations with your own ideas. Then take turns asking and answering the questions with a partner.**

1. *A* Do you think people spend too much time worrying about being happy?
   B Well, as far as I'm concerned, _____ .

2. *A* Do you think people believe having lots of money will make them happy?
   B Good question. As far as I know, _____ .

3. *A* Do you think having a successful career is overrated?
   B You know, as far as I can tell, _____ .

3 Strategies What makes people unhappy?

A **CD 3.34** **Listen to the conversations. Write the expressions you hear. Then practice with a partner.**

1. *A* Would having a long commute make you unhappy, do you think?
   B Maybe. Sitting in traffic is the worst thing, _____ .
   A Because I read that _____ commuting, people who have to travel one hour to work each day need to earn 40 percent more to be as happy as people who walk to work.

2. *A* Is it true that people are less happy when there's an economic recession?
   B I'd say so. I mean, _____ jobs, there's less work going around, and people get laid off.
   A Right. But there are fewer divorces during a recession, _____ . Why is that?
   B Well, _____ , it's because people can't afford to get divorced!

3. *A* Do you think that people who live in big cities are happy? _____ , it's stressful to live with like, 15 million other people.
   B Yeah. _____ , living in a small town is better. I mean, _____ stress.
   A Though _____ culture _____ , there are a lot more things going on in a big city, I guess.

About you | **B** Pair work **Take turns asking and answering the questions in Exercise A. Give your own answers.**

C Group work **What other things make people unhappy, do you think? Discuss your ideas. Can you agree on the five most common things that make people unhappy?**

"As far as I can tell, there are lots of things that make people unhappy, like having no friends."

4 Speaking naturally Stress in expressions *See page 142.*

Lesson D *The politics of happiness*

① Reading

A **Prepare** What factors make a country "happy"? Brainstorm a list of ideas.

"I would think that wealth is one factor. People in rich countries must be happy."

B ⬇ **Read for main ideas** Read the article. How many of your ideas are mentioned?

Unhappy?
Maybe you're not in the right country!

China

Bhutan

India

1 If you're not feeling as happy as you'd like, maybe you should consider moving to another country – like Denmark, for example. According to social psychologist Adrian White, who analyzed data and surveys of 80,000 people in 178 countries, Denmark is the happiest nation in the world, closely followed by its northern European neighbors Finland, Norway, and the Netherlands.

2 Not surprisingly, perhaps, the happiest countries are also the healthiest and wealthiest and those that provide their citizens with a good level of education. People may pay high taxes in these countries, but they are rewarded with other benefits such as shorter work weeks, as well as more vacation time. All of these contribute to a general sense of well-being. Size also matters. Smaller countries, which have a strong sense of national identity and social cohesion, rate better in terms of happiness than countries with larger populations.

3 While the governments of many countries seek to increase wealth and prosperity for their citizens, at least one government has made its citizens' happiness a priority. In Bhutan, a tiny country between China and India, happiness is part of government policy. Instead of measuring GNP (Gross National Product), Bhutan measures GNH (Gross National Happiness). Their rationale is that by putting a high value on health, education, and general well-being, citizens' lives will be improved in ways that enrich their nation's environment and culture. The program seems to be working: 19 percent of Bhutan's inhabitants live below the poverty level, yet only 4 percent of the population claim to be unhappy.

4 There could well be lessons here for other governments hoping to improve both their GNP and GNH. Happier people tend to be more productive, leading to greater economic wealth. Moreover, they are often healthier, resulting in lower spending on health care. Ideas for producing happier citizens might include reducing unemployment – a major cause of unhappiness – improving parenting skills to create happier families, and finding ways to stimulate kindness toward others, which is known to make both the givers and receivers happier. In Japan, for example, "community credit" programs encourage couples who live too far from their aging parents to "adopt" an elderly person locally to care for. By doing this, they can earn credits that their own parents can use to "buy" similar volunteer care in their own neighborhoods. Governments adopting such programs might well see both the happiness and wealth of their nations improve.

5 Of course, neither relocating to a new country nor waiting for new government policies may be the best way to guarantee your future happiness. Fortunately, however, researchers are coming to the conclusion that the main ingredient for a happy life is love. And that's something that no government can help you with.

C Reading for detail Do the statements below agree with the information in the article? Write Y (Yes), N (No), or NG (Information not given).

1. All European countries are happy. _____
2. Education contributes to a nation's well-being. _____
3. Most of Bhutan's population lives above the poverty level. _____
4. Wealth makes people happy, according to the research. _____
5. There are good economic reasons for governments to make citizens happier. _____
6. In Japan, there are programs to help people become better parents. _____

About you

D Pair work React Discuss the questions.

• What do you think of the idea that governments can be responsible for your happiness? Whose responsibility is it to make people happy, do you think?
• Do you think you live in a happy country? Why? Why not?
• What could be changed in your country to make people happier?

② Focus on vocabulary Synonyms

A Find a word in the article with a similar meaning to replace each word or expression in bold. Change its form, if necessary. The paragraph numbers are given.

What do governments do?

Analyze

1. **Study** economic trends. (para. 1)
2. Collect taxes from the country's **people**. (3 possible answers) (para. 2, 3)
3. Decide the **most important things** for the **country**. (para. 3, 1)
4. Develop **plans** for how the country operates. (para. 3)
5. **Try to find** ways to make the country **richer**. (para. 3, 2)
6. **Encourage** economic growth. (para. 4)

About you

B Pair work Use each word from Exercise A to describe other things that governments do.

"One thing the government is doing at the moment is analyzing the banking industry."

③ Listening and speaking Happiness and the community

A ◀))) CD 3.37 Read the sentences from a handout for a sociology class. Guess the missing words. Then listen to part of a lecture, and complete each sentence with no more than three words.

1. There's evidence that people in richer areas are _____ people in poorer areas.
2. Furthermore, research suggests that in _____ people are less happy.
3. Happiness is a good thing. Happy people _____ , and they are also healthier.
4. In addition, happy people tend to be good citizens and _____ to their communities.

B ◀))) CD 3.38 Listen to more of the lecture. Write the three proposals that the lecturer suggests can make communities happier.

1. _____
2. _____
3. _____

About you

C Pair work What do you think of the ideas in Exercise B? Can you agree on three policies that would make your community a happier place?

Writing *Policies for happiness*

In this lesson, you . . .
- answer an essay question.
- add ideas with *as well as*, etc.
- avoid errors with *in addition to*, etc.

Task | **Write a paragraph in an essay.**

Should a government try to make its citizens happy?
How? Give specific reasons and examples.

A **Look at a model** Read this paragraph from an essay. What is the student's answer to the first question above? What reasons does the student give? What other reasons can you think of?

> As far as governments are concerned, there are several good economic reasons for having policies that make citizens happy. First, happiness is important to the economy because happy workers are more effective, (as well as) more productive. In addition, research shows that happy people contribute more to their community in terms of volunteering. Furthermore, happy people tend to be healthier, which means that they cost less in terms of health care. Every government should try to increase citizens' happiness in addition to stimulating economic growth in other ways.

B **Focus on language** Look at the paragraph again. How does the student add ideas? Circle three more expressions (not including *and*). Then read the grammar chart.

Adding ideas in writing

You can use *as well as* and *in addition to* to add ideas within a sentence.
As well as mostly connects noun phrases and adjectives.
Happy workers are more effective, **as well as** *more productive.*

In addition to mostly connects noun phrases. Use an *-ing* form to add a verb.
Governments can increase happiness **in addition to** *(stimulating) economic growth.*

In addition, furthermore, and *moreover* add ideas to a previous sentence.
Happy people are productive. **In addition**, *they contribute more to their community.*

Writing vs. Conversation

Moreover and *furthermore* are mostly used in formal writing and formal speaking.

C **Rewrite the sentences, replacing the words in bold with the expressions given. Make any necessary changes to punctuation or grammar. Then compare with a partner.**

1. Governments can have an effect on people's health. **Also**, they can affect their well-being. (In addition)
2. Some governments measure their nation's happiness **and** their GNP. (as well as)
3. Happy people take fewer sick days. **Also**, they tend to be more productive at work. (Furthermore)
4. An economic recession is bad for a country. It makes people unhappy, **too**. (Moreover)
5. People in happier countries have a shorter work week **and** they get more vacation time. (in addition to)
6. People are responsible for their own health **and** for creating their own happiness. (in addition to)

D **Write and check** Now write your own paragraph for the essay question. Then check for errors.

Common errors

Remember to use an *-ing* form after a preposition.
It makes us happier in addition to **making** *us richer.* (NOT . . . *in addition to* ~~make~~ . . .)
Don't use *as well as* to connect a clause with a new subject.
This increases happiness as well as **stimulating** *wealth.* (NOT . . . ~~it stimulates . . .~~)

Vocabulary notebook *Get started!*

I have a lot of homework, and a friend calls and asks me to go out. "I'm sorry. I can't go out with you tonight. I really need to <u>get started</u> on my homework."

A **Read the situations below. Complete the things you can say using the expressions in the box. Write the correct forms of *get*.**

| get (me) down | get anywhere | get in the way | get it off the ground | get on with | get to be |

1. My friend and I just started a small business, but it's not easy.
   "It's not easy _____ ."

2. I just finished practicing my violin, and I managed to play a more difficult piece.
   "It's definitely _____ easier."

3. I had a lot of problems with my ex-girlfriend last year.
   "It was really _____ . I often felt very depressed."

4. I have a lot of homework, and it's affecting my free time.
   "All this work is _____ of my social life!"

5. I'm trying to write a paper, and I'm not making any progress.
   "I'm not _____ with this!"

6. My best friend just got divorced.
   "He just wants to _____ his life."

B **Now write your own situations and things you can say for these expressions.**

1. get ahead _____
   " _____ ."

2. get off to a good start _____
   " _____ ."

3. get under way _____
   " _____ ."

4. get to the top _____
   " _____ ."

C **Word builder What do these *get* expressions mean? Write a situation and something you can say for each one.**

1. I like to **get my own way**.
2. I didn't **get a lot out of** it.
3. I couldn't **get through to** him.
4. I wanted to **get involved** in the project.
5. I just **got carried away**.
6. I can't **get it together**.

It's probably hard for her to get on with her life after her divorce.

On your own

Find a celebrity magazine. What can you say about each celebrity? Annotate the photos using *get* expressions from the lesson.

Checkpoint 3 *Units 7–9*

1 Childhood memories

A Rewrite these memories in your notebook. Use an *-ing* form to rewrite the underlined sentences. Replace the words in parentheses with a correct form of a phrasal verb in the box.

clean up	come up with	give up	have over	put off	run out of
come up	give back	go over	✓ look forward to	put up with	wake up

1. I was always the first person home after school. <u>I used to sit by the window and wait for my mom to get home from work.</u> I (couldn't wait) seeing her car in the driveway.

   I was always the first person home after school. I used to sit by the window, waiting for my mom to get home from work. I looked forward to seeing her car in the driveway.

2. During summer vacations, I'd (invite . . . over) my friends for play dates. <u>There were always kids who played at our house.</u> If we made a big mess, my mom always (tolerated) it. She (made it clean) afterward, too!

3. I always found homework difficult. I'd (postpone) doing it. Or I'd just (stop). My dad would always (check, read) it with me. He helped me with any problems that (appeared). <u>I used to listen to him and think he was the smartest guy.</u>

4. My grandma was always (thinking of) fun things to do. She never (stopped having) ideas! <u>I remember that I played with her for hours.</u>

5. My sister was always taking my things. She never (returned them), either! And she'd (stop me sleeping) early. <u>The fact that I had to get up early was the worst.</u>

About you **B** **Pair work** Take turns telling stories from your childhood. Use expressions like *honestly*, *frankly*, *to be honest*, and *to tell you the truth* to make your statements stronger.

"When I came home after school, my mom was always there. I have to say, I loved that."

2 Happiness and politics

A Complete the comments with *all, both, each, every, neither, no*, and *none*. Use *of* when necessary. Sometimes there is more than one correct answer.

1. In some countries, ___all___ college education is free. _____ student should get that, so they don't have huge college bills to pay off.

2. _____ country should have a policy to make _____ their citizens happy. Unfortunately, _____ the countries in this region do that.

3. _____ family should pay for their own health care. It's your own responsibility.

4. Many people have _____ formal job training. _____ employee should get training.

5. _____ government wants its economy to fail. When there are _____ jobs, the priority should be to stimulate the economy and create new jobs.

6. Denmark and Finland are two of the happiest nations. _____ countries spend a lot on education. _____ country has good health care, too. However, _____ these countries has low taxes!

About you **B** **Pair work** Discuss the views in Exercise A. Do you agree with each other? Use expressions like *in other words, what I mean is*, and *I'm not saying* to make your meaning clear.

Healthy living

A Complete the sentences with a correct form of the verbs given. Use *from* when necessary. Then circle the correct words to complete the comments.

1. It's probably good for you ___to drink___ (drink) milk. It may strengthen your **teeth / metabolism**. It might also prevent your **bones / liver** _____ (break).

2. It can be bad for some people _____ (eat) too much meat. But fish may stop you _____ (get) **heart disease / immune system**. It may also be good for your **brain / muscles** because it helps your memory.

3. It's probably not healthy _____ (eat) too much salt. In some cases it might cause your **blood pressure / digestive system** _____ (rise).

4. Make sure there's always fruit _____ (snack on) in the fridge. Fruit like blueberries can help you _____ (concentrate). And some research shows kiwis can keep your **skin / eyesight** _____ (deteriorate).

5. We always had vegetables _____ (eat) at school. And I've always enjoyed _____ (eat) them, actually, which is good. I mean, they can protect you _____ (get) all kinds of diseases. And putting avocados on your **skin / muscles** can make it _____ (feel) really soft.

6. It's worth _____ (teach) kids about food. My family always has fun _____ (cook) together.

7. I've never had any trouble _____ (watch) my weight. I eat chili peppers, and I read they enable some people _____ (lose) weight. I think they increase your **metabolism / liver**.

About you

B Pair work Discuss the comments in Exercise A. Use the expressions in the box.

When it comes to . . . ,	in terms of . . .	As far as I know,	As far as I can tell,
As far as . . . go / goes *or* is / are concerned,		As far as I'm concerned,	

"As far as milk is concerned, I know it's good for you, but it's not a big part of my diet."

Expectations

A Circle the correct *get* expressions in the conversation. Then rewrite the sentences, changing the verbs in *italics* to the passive form.

Young people are expected . . .

A We *expect* young people to achieve so much. They need a good degree to get **ahead** / **down**.

B I know. They feel they have to get **to be** / **to the top** in their careers. Or they think people *won't see* them as successful. They*'ve done* a lot of research on the pressure this causes. It gets people **down** / **off** to a bad start. It's really getting **off the ground** / **to be** a national problem.

A Yeah. Over 20 companies *rejected* one of my friends. She couldn't get **in the way** / **anywhere** with her career. She just wanted to get a job and to get **on with** / **under way** her life.

B Yeah. They *should do* something about unemployment. I mean, parents *are going to support* their adult children a lot more. Parents just want their kids to get **under way** / **off** to a good start.

About you

B Pair work Discuss the topic in Exercise A. Use expressions like *take, like,* and *for instance* to give examples from your life. Use rhetorical questions to make a point.

"I think we are expected to achieve a lot. For instance, you have to get work experience and a degree. I mean, why do we have to have work experience before we get a job?"

Going places

10

In Unit 10, you . . .

- talk about travel and vacations.
- learn more about reported speech and reported thought.
- draw conclusions from things people say.
- use *In what way?* to ask for details.

Lesson A *Travel blog*

1 Vocabulary in context

A 🔊 CD 4.02 **Look at the pictures. What can you guess about Rob's trip? Then read the blog and check your guesses.**

Rob's *Amazon* travel blog

Days 21 and 22: Bolivia – to Rurrenabaque via La Paz

The first views of La Paz were **amazing** – **impressive** downtown buildings surrounded by vast suburbs climbing up breathtaking mountains; the trip was **fascinating** but **tiring**. I slept well that night. The next morning, I asked about travel to Rurrenabaque, gateway to the Amazon Basin. The tour agent informed me that the last bus had left. She also said the trip would take an **exhausting** 18 hours or more by bus – a **depressing** thought – so I opted to fly despite the cost. I called the airport; they said all the flights that day were full. They told me there were seats on the 6:00 a.m. flight the next day, which meant getting up at 4:00 a.m.! So I went to the airport the following

morning. I was **puzzled** that only a handful of people were checking in, which was **surprising**, since Rurrenabaque is a popular destination. I soon discovered why. The check-in agent explained that the plane was just a 16-seater – a **frightening** prospect. Then she said there might be a delay because of bad weather, which wasn't very **encouraging**. In the end, the flight was on time, though I have to say it was pretty **challenging**. The pilot warned us that the landing would be really bumpy – and it was! Actually, it was **terrifying**. I was just happy to get there safely, and I felt much more **relaxed** in the evening. It was the start of my Amazon adventure!

B **Answer the questions. Underline the words in the blog that give you the answers.**

When did Rob feel . . . a. tired? b. depressed? c. surprised? d. terrified?

Word sort

C **Make a chart like this of the adjectives in bold in the blog. Add the other adjective and verb forms.**

You feel . . .	because something is . . .	The verb is . . .
amazed	amazing	amaze

Vocabulary notebook
See page 115.

About you

D **Pair work** Talk about travel experiences you have had. Take turns using words from your charts.

"I flew in bad weather once. It was pretty frightening. Actually, I was terrified."

2 Grammar Reporting what people say

Figure it out

A Read the things below that people said to Rob. Write how he reports them in his blog. How are the reports different from the words the people actually used? Then read the grammar chart.

1. "There are seats on the 6:00 a.m. flight tomorrow." 2. "There may be a delay."

Reported speech: statements

Grammar extra
See page 162.

When you report things people said in the past, the verb tense often "shifts back."

"The plane**'s** just a 16-seater." → The agent explained (that) the plane **was** just a 16-seater.
"The last bus **has left**." → She informed me (that) the last bus **had left**.

These modal verbs change in reported speech: *can* → *could*; *will* → *would*; *may* → *might*; *must* → *had to*. "There **may** be a delay." → She said (that) there **might** be a delay.	These modal verbs don't change: *could, should, would, might, used to.*

Time expressions often change, too.

"The flights are full **today** and **tomorrow**."
→ He said the flights were full **that day** and **the next day**.

Common errors

Use an indirect object after *tell*, but not after *explain* or *say*.
He told **me** the flight was full. (NOT ~~He told the . . .~~)
He explained/said the flight was full. (NOT ~~He explained/said me . . .~~)

B In Rurrenabaque Rob met up with Conrad, who had been there before. Complete the reported speech from the rest of Rob's blog. Add *me* where necessary.

1. "We can take a boat trip on the Beni River tomorrow." *Conrad said . . .*
2. "We'll see some amazing wildlife." *He told . . .*
3. "We must make a reservation today." *He explained . . .*
4. "I saw some monkeys, and we may even see pink dolphins." *He said . . .*
5. "People used to leave trash in the forests." *He explained . . .*
6. "Tour companies have become more aware of the environment." *He told . . .*
7. "We should go on a guided tour today so we can learn all about the rain forest." *He said . . .*

C Pair work Close your books. Take turns remembering the things that Conrad said.

"Conrad said they could take a boat trip on the Beni River the next day."

3 Listening and speaking More adventures in Bolivia

A ◄)) CD 4.03 Listen. Natalie talks about things you can do in Bolivia. Number the photos 1–5.

Eduardo Avaroa National Park   Oruro   Lake Titicaca   La Paz   Huayna Potosí

B ◄)) CD 4.04 Listen again. Describe what you can do in each place, using no more than four words.

About you

C Group work What interesting travel destinations have you been told about? Tell your group.

"My friend José told me Cairo was a great place to go. He said the museums were fascinating."

Lesson B *I never travel without it!*

1 Grammar in context

A Look at the pictures. Why do you think people might take these things on a trip?

"Well, an eye mask and earplugs would be useful on a long flight. Otherwise, it's hard to sleep."

an eye mask and earplugs

a flashlight

shampoo and conditioner

a scented candle

family photos

green tea

B ◀))) CD 4.05 **Read the article. Complete each comment with one of the items above.**

We asked six experienced travelers what special items they take with them on a trip.

"People I meet often ask me whether I'm married or have any kids, so I always have a few _____ to show them." **Carl, Los Angeles**

"I find traveling so exhausting. A friend told me to try _____ . It energizes you. I always take some with me now."
Hugo, Mexico City

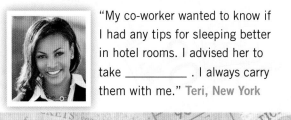

"My co-worker wanted to know if I had any tips for sleeping better in hotel rooms. I advised her to take _____ . I always carry them with me." **Teri, New York**

"People often ask me why I always take _____ with me when I travel. It makes a hotel room feel more like home." **Hae-won, Seoul**

"My sister asked me to lend her _____ for a road trip she was taking. Up until then, it had never occurred to me how useful it could be – especially if you go out at night and there are no streetlights. So now I always take one with me." **Erkan, Istanbul**

"My own favorite _____ . A friend of mine who's a hairstylist told me not to use the ones that you find in cheap hotels. They can damage your hair." **Raquel, San Juan**

About you

C **Pair work** **What would you never travel without? Why? Tell a partner.**

A I'd never go away without music to listen to. Traveling can be so boring, even on a short bus trip.
B Me neither. And I would never travel without my e-reader.

2 Grammar Reporting what people ask and instruct

Figure it out

A How do the speakers in the article report the things that people said to them? Underline the places in the article that give you the answers. Then read the grammar chart.

1. "Are you married?"
2. "Why do you always take a scented candle?"
3. "Try green tea."

Grammar extra See page 163.

Reported speech: questions and instructions

Reported questions use the word order of statements. They do not have question marks.
"Are you married?" → People often ask me **whether/if I'm** married.
"What do you take with you?" → We asked people **what they take/took** with them.
"Why shouldn't I use hotel shampoo?" → She asked me **why she shouldn't use** hotel shampoo.

You do not need to "shift back" the verb tense when you report information about the present or future that is still true or relevant.
"Do you have any kids?" "I have two." → A woman asked me if I **have** kids. I told her I **have** two.
"Where are you going on your next trip?" → He wanted to know where I**'m going** on my next trip.

Use an infinitive after *ask, tell, order, advise* to report a request, a suggestion, or an instruction.
"Can you lend me a flashlight?" → My sister asked me **to lend** her a flashlight.
"Don't use hotel shampoo." → A friend told/advised me **not to use** hotel shampoo.

In conversation . . .
Ask . . . *if* is more common in conversation than *ask . . . whether.*

B Lucy and her friend Sally are packing for a trip. Look at what Sally says, and complete the reports. Which reports might be different after they get back?

1. "Are you taking your running shoes?"   Sally asked Lucy _____ .
2. "Put the shoes in a plastic bag."   She told her _____ .
3. "Why do you always take a pillow?"   Sally wanted to know _____ .
4. "Does it have to be that pillow?"   She asked Lucy _____ .
5. "Don't pack too much stuff."   Sally advised her _____ .
6. "How many bags are you taking?"   Sally wanted to know _____ .

3 Viewpoint Get ready for a trip.

A **Pair work** Imagine you are going on a bus tour. Ask about six things that your partner plans to take. Ask your partner to do three things for you.

A *Are you taking something to read?*
B *Yeah. I think I might download some new books.*
A *Can you recommend a book in English that's not too hard?*

The tour company said they would provide everything but the kitchen sink.

TOUR BUS

DONNELLY

B **Pair work** Tell another classmate the questions your first partner asked, and what he or she asked you to do.

"Nela asked me if I was taking something to read. I said I might download some new books. She asked me to recommend a book for her."

4 Speaking naturally Silent vowels *See page 142.*

Lesson C *So what you're saying is . . .*

 1 **Conversation strategy** Drawing conclusions

A Look at the advertisement from a website. Do you think space tourism will ever become popular? Would it appeal to you? Why? Why not?

> **Book your place in space, and go on the voyage of a lifetime . . .**
>
> - Travel at three times the speed of sound (2,500 mph / 4,000 kph).
> - Experience the sensation of total silence 68 miles (110 km) above the earth.
> - Feel the freedom of being weightless as you float in the air.

B ◀))) CD 4.08 **Listen. What does Wen think about going into space? How about Hai-Fang?**

Wen	I read this article that said people would be taking vacations in space within a couple of decades. Can you imagine going into space? It would be such a weird sensation.
Hai-Fang	Weird in what way? Isn't it just like being on a plane, only higher up?
Wen	Yeah, but imagine being weightless and floating around.
Hai-Fang	Oh, you mean eating your lunch upside down? Yeah, that would be weird.
Wen	But it'd be fascinating – like the trip of a lifetime. A voyage into the unknown.
Hai-Fang	So what you're saying is you could live out your *Star Trek* fantasy. Hmm. I think I'd prefer to keep my feet on the ground.
Wen	So I guess you won't be coming, then, when I blast off into outer space?
Hai-Fang	I doubt it. You know I don't even like roller coasters!

C **Notice** how Hai-Fang and Wen draw conclusions from what the other one says using expressions like these. Find examples in the conversation.

> *you mean . . .*
> *(so) you're saying (that) . . .*
> *(so) what you're saying is . . .*
> *(so) I guess . . . (then)*

D Complete the rest of the conversation with the expressions above. Then practice. Do you agree with the views? Discuss with a partner.

Hai-Fang . . . Yeah, I just don't think going into space would be my thing.

Wen _____ you'd find it too scary?

Hai-Fang Yeah. Imagine being in a tiny cabin with no chance of escaping in an emergency!

Wen _____ it's just not worth the risk, then.

Hai-Fang Exactly.

Wen _____ you'd never go bungee jumping or skydiving?

Hai-Fang No way.

110 Unit 10: Going places

2 Strategy plus *In what way?*

It'd be such a weird experience.

Weird **in what way?**

◀)) CD 4.09 You can use *In what way?* to ask for more details about someone's ideas or opinions.

A ◀)) CD 4.10 **Listen to the start of five conversations. How does each one continue? Write the letters a–e.**

1. Eating meals in space would be so weird. _____
2. Space travel must be bad for the environment. _____
3. Going into space would be terrifying. _____
4. Sitting in a tiny cabin would be frustrating. _____
5. A space vacation would be life-changing. _____

a. I'd want to be outside doing a space walk.
b. You can't escape if something goes wrong.
c. You'd never look at things in the same way again.
d. Well, for one thing, it pollutes the atmosphere.
e. Well, imagine your pizza floating around!

B ◀)) CD 4.11 **Now listen to the complete conversations, and check your answers. Then practice with a partner. Can you continue the conversations?**

3 Strategies A different travel experience

A **Fill in the first two blanks in each conversation with expressions from the lesson. Then choose a comment in the box to complete each conversation. Practice.**

> You'd have to trust the pilot and hope you landed safely!
> It would be like spending your vacation in prison.
> An adventure is something that just *happens*. Nobody organizes it.

1. *A* Some scuba divers did an underwater vacation for two weeks! Wouldn't that be just terrifying?
   B Terrifying _____ ?
   A Well, I think I would just panic all the time. I wouldn't enjoy one minute of it.
   B _____ you'd be scared?
   A Exactly. _____

2. *A* You know, I think adventure travel must be a bit boring.
   B I'm not sure what you mean. Boring _____ ?
   A Well, someone else organizing your vacation isn't really an *adventure*, is it?
   B _____ an adventure is something you organize yourself?
   A No. _____

3. *A* I think going up in a hot-air balloon would be quite challenging.
   B _____ it would be an unpleasant experience?
   A No, I just mean it would be . . . well . . . challenging.
   B But challenging _____ ?
   A _____

About you

B **Pair work** **Practice the conversations in Exercise A again, giving your opinions. Then take turns starting conversations about different kinds of unusual trips.**

A My friend said she'd been on safari. She said it was a bit scary.
B Scary in what way?

Lesson D *Global tourism*

1 Reading

A **Prepare** Is tourism a big industry in your country? If so, in which areas?

"We get a lot of tourists here. One of the most popular places is . . ."

B  **Read for main ideas** Read the article. How big is the tourist industry? What are the challenges for the agencies that manage tourism?

The tourist threat

[1] Tourism is one of the world's largest industries. According to the World Travel and Tourism Council, it's a $2 trillion business that directly accounts for almost 1 in 11 jobs globally. Worldwide, many countries have come to rely heavily on tourism as an important part of their economy, while other countries – such as some of the smaller Caribbean island nations – are almost completely dependent on tourism for their survival.

[2] Despite its economic benefits, tourism has a downside, too. While countries eagerly spend millions attracting tourists to their shores, they are also struggling with the negative impacts that tourism brings with it.

[3] One of the biggest threats is environmental. The building of roads, hotels, and resorts can quickly destroy those very beautiful landscapes on which tourism depends in the first place. Development on wetlands, for example, impacts wildlife; forests disappear as they are cleared to make way for buildings and to provide fuel.

[4] In addition, the tourist industry also puts a huge pressure on scarce water supplies. In dry Mediterranean areas, tourists using leisure facilities like swimming pools and golf courses consume almost twice as much water as local residents.

[5] Tourism accounts for about 60 percent of air travel and creates noise and air pollution, which have negative effects on the environment. In Yosemite National Park, in the U.S., the number of roads and parking lots has increased so much to keep pace with the growing number of visitors that smog is now adversely affecting the wildlife and vegetation.

[6] Tourism is also responsible for producing huge amounts of waste. Cruise ships in the Caribbean generate a lot of trash – more than 70,000 tons each year. It even affects remote regions like the Himalayas, where Everest, the world's highest mountain, has more than 100 tons of trash sitting on its slopes and peaks.

[7] In spite of these problems, responsibly managed tourism can bring many positive benefits to communities and the environment. Revenues from park-entrance fees pay for the protection of sensitive areas – or in Borneo for the care of young orangutans. Income from departure taxes in Belize covers some of the costs of conserving the reefs.

[8] Furthermore, tourism brings people into close contact with natural areas like rain forests, and can give them a better understanding of the environment and the consequences of destroying it. This awareness can lead to pressure on local governments to preserve these beautiful areas, and can result in the protection of endangered plants and animals.

[9] A further positive effect of tourism is that it can lead to alternate employment opportunities. In Guatemala, Spanish-language schools for tourists now hire local people who were previously employed in industries such as hunting and deforestation.

[10] Although tourism has many positive benefits, it clearly has a negative impact as well. The challenge for local and national agencies is to manage tourism so that communities can benefit economically, and yet at the same time, make sure that the tourist areas are preserved for all to enjoy.

Reading tip

The final paragraph of a long article often gives a short summary of the whole article.

C Read for topic The writer of the article mentions a number of effects that tourism has. Which four of these effects are mentioned? Check (✔) the boxes.

☐ Deforestation to provide fuel   ☐ Atmospheric pollution from transportation
☐ Stress on water resources   ☐ Damage to plants from hikers
☐ Poor planning of buildings and facilities   ☐ Littering of tourist areas

D Read for evidence Read the article again to find these things. Then discuss your own views on tourism with a partner, using the information to help you build your argument.

- three statistics that show the economic importance of tourism
- five specific examples of how tourism has affected places negatively
- two examples of how tourist dollars can help a country
- an example of how tourism stops people harming the environment

"Tourism is important in terms of employment, and it says here that about 10 percent of the global workforce works in tourism somehow."

② Focus on vocabulary Synonyms

A Find the words in bold in the article. Then find words with similar meanings in the same paragraph. Use them to rewrite the sentences below, making any changes necessary.

businesses
1. Tourism is one of the biggest **industries** here.
2. Some areas **are almost completely dependent on** tourism.
3. The **building** of tourist resorts has had a huge impact on the environment.
4. Air pollution and noise have **negative effects on** the wildlife.
5. Tourists **generate a lot of trash**.
6. **Income** from tourism has helped protect endangered plants and animals.
7. People have a greater **awareness** of environmental issues, which can **result in** better protection of the environment.
8. Hotels and other businesses **hire** local people, which benefits local communities.

About you   **B** Pair work Which sentences are true for your country? Discuss and give examples.

"Tourism is definitely one of the biggest businesses here. It's an important industry in . . ."

③ Listening and speaking Responsible tourism

A Pair work Look at the tourist pamphlet on the right. Think of different ways to complete the sentences.

B 🔊 CD 4.12 Listen to a short presentation by an eco-tour guide. Complete the sentences in the pamphlet.

C 🔊 CD 4.13 Listen again. Answer the questions.

1. What two reasons does the guide give for shopping at local markets?
2. Why does the guide encourage people not to bargain?
3. What story does the guide tell about a tourist who bought coral?

About you   **D** Pair work Agree on the five most important things that people can do to be responsible tourists. Prepare a short presentation for tourists. Take turns presenting to the class.

> **How to be a responsible tourist . . .**
>
> 1. Choose a tour company that does not _____ .
> 2. Stay in a place that _____ .
> 3. Save _____ .
> 4. Buy _____ .
> 5. When you buy things, pay _____ .
> 6. Ask before _____ .

Writing *Are tourists welcome?*

In this lesson, you . . .
- write up your survey notes.
- contrast ideas with *although*, etc.
- avoid errors with *although*.

Task Write a survey article.

Are tourists a good or bad thing?

A **Brainstorm** Ask your classmates the question above, and take notes on their views. Then compare with a partner.

"Maria thinks tourism is a bad thing. She said she'd left a museum once because of all the tourists."

B **Look at the models** Read the extracts from two articles in a student magazine. Complete the last sentence in each extract with one of your own ideas.

Tourists are a nuisance!

Tourism brings a number of benefits to our community. It creates employment and strengthens the local economy. However, my survey shows that residents have mixed feelings about its impact. Although tourism has its advantages, many people feel that large groups of tourists are a nuisance. In fact, most people said they would prefer the tourists to stay away despite the jobs that tourism creates. When I asked one person why he held this view, he said . . .

Tourists are a good thing . . .

With the growth in tourism, I asked local students whether tourism brought problems or benefits. Interestingly enough, even though many people find tourists annoying, the view of most is that the advantages of tourism outweigh the disadvantages. It is true that tourists leave litter and crowd the streets. Nevertheless, most people welcome tourists to the region. We need them in spite of the problems they create. One person said . . .

C **Focus on language** Circle five more expressions in the extracts in Exercise B that contrast ideas. Then read the grammar chart.

Contrasting ideas in writing

Use *although* and *even though* to connect clauses.
Although / Even though *tourism creates jobs, it has disadvantages.*
Tourism is a good thing, ***although / even though*** *it brings problems.*

Use *despite* and *in spite of* before noun phrases or *-ing* forms.
Despite / In spite of *(causing) problems, tourists are welcome.*
Tourism can be good ***despite / in spite of*** *the problems it causes.*

Nevertheless, like *however*, contrasts an idea in a previous sentence.
Tourists may bring problems. ***Nevertheless***, *people welcome them.*

Writing vs. Conversation

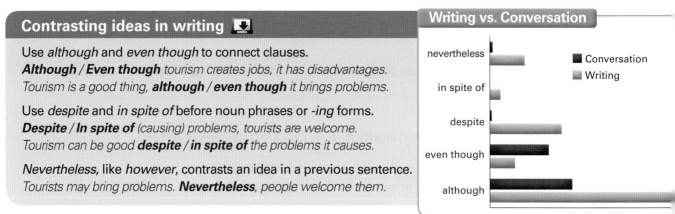

D **Circle the correct expressions to complete the sentences.**

1. **Although / Despite** groups of tourists can be annoying, tourism is important to the local economy.
2. You can still enjoy the sights in the city, **in spite of / although** the crowds of tourists.
3. Tourism creates employment, **even though / despite** many of the jobs are low paid.
4. Tourism can damage the environment. **Despite / Nevertheless**, resorts are still being developed.

E **Write and check** Write your article. Include your classmates' views. Then check for errors.

Common errors

Use *despite / in spite of* before a noun phrase. Avoid *although*.
Despite *the problems, tourism has benefits.* (NOT ~~Although~~ *the problems, tourism . . .*)

Vocabulary notebook *So amazing!*

Learning tip   **Word forks**

When you learn a new word, find other words in the same word family – for example, the noun(s), verb(s), adjective(s). Make word forks. You can add example sentences.

frighten
- verb **to frighten** *Flying frightens me.*
- adj **frightening** *The flight was frightening.*
- adj **frightened** *I felt frightened during takeoff.*
- noun **fright** *I had a terrible fright.*

A Complete the word forks with verb and adjective forms.

1.

amaze
- | verb   When I arrived, the city __amazed__ me.
- | ____   The architecture was _____ .
- | adj   I was _____ when I saw the buildings.

2.

fascinate
- | verb   Rome has always _____ me.
- | adj   Rome is a _____ city.
- | ____   I'm always _____ just to watch the people there.

3.

impress
- | ____   What _____ me most was the beach.
- | ____   The beach was _____ .
- | ____   The beach was clean, which _____ me.

4.

terrify
- | ____   What _____ me is sailing.
- | ____   I think the ocean is _____ .
- | ____   I'm _____ when I get on a boat.

Dictionary tip

Read the example sentences in a dictionary to see how each form of a word is used.

> surprise
> *noun* [C/U]
> *I want the party to be **a surprise**.*
> ***To my great surprise,** they gave us what we asked for.*

B Think of trips you have made. Use your own ideas to create word forks for these verbs.

1.

depress
- | ____   _____
- | ____   _____
- | ____   _____

2.

encourage
- | ____   _____
- | ____   _____
- | ____   _____

3.

exhaust
- | ____   _____
- | ____   _____
- | ____   _____

4.

relax
- | ____   _____
- | ____   _____
- | ____   _____

C Word builder What are the noun forms of the verbs in Exercises A and B? Add them to the word forks. Use a dictionary to help you write example sentences.

The museums are fascinating.

On your own

Write a travel blog for a place that you have visited or know well. Add photos.

Culture

In Unit 11, you . . .

- talk about weddings, gifts, and traditions.
- use relative clauses with *when*, *where*, *whose*.
- use verbs with two objects.
- soften comments with expressions like *a little*.
- say *Yeah, no* to agree and make a comment.

Lesson A *Weddings*

1 Vocabulary in context

A 🔊 CD 4.14 **Think of ten words associated with weddings. Then read the postings on this web page. How many of your words are mentioned?**

Write a new post

▶ When is a good time to get married?

Björn The best time here in Sweden is the summer, when it stays light all night.

Ming Wei It depends. Here it's often decided by a fortune-teller, whose job is to choose the best day.

Alex Any weekend when you can get off work. :-)

▶ What's your favorite part of the wedding?

Rodrigo There's a very touching moment when the bride **walks down the aisle** with her **bridesmaids**, and the **groom** turns and sees her in her wedding dress for the first time.

Gosia My favorite part is when they **go to the reception**, where the couple is met by their parents. The parents give the newlyweds a gift of bread and salt, which in Poland symbolize the prosperity and hardship of life.

Manuel It's when the bride and groom **exchange vows**.

▶ How have weddings changed in recent years?

Kumiko There was a time when weddings were very traditional in Japan, but that changed in the 1980s, when **Western-style ceremonies** became more popular.

Jun Ho Here in South Korea, marriages were traditionally arranged by a **matchmaker**, whose responsibility was to find the right partner for you. I have lots of friends whose parents met that way, but **arranged marriages** aren't as common nowadays.

Cassidy There aren't as many **religious ceremonies**. Some people go to Hawaii, where they get married on the beach, or there are actually places in the States where a celebrity look-alike, like Elvis, **performs a civil ceremony**.

Chris They go on longer. They have all these **bachelor and bachelorette parties** now, where you celebrate with your friends. Sometimes they go on all night, and some last the whole weekend. Then there's the **rehearsal dinner**, where the **parents of the groom host a dinner** for everybody who's involved – the bridesmaids, the **best man**, and **groomsmen**.

Word sort

B **Make a chart like the one below. Use the words in bold from the postings.**

Types of weddings	People involved	Things people do
Western-style ceremony	bride	walk down the aisle

Vocabulary notebook

See page 125.

About you

C **Pair work** Take turns using the words in the chart to ask questions about the postings. How much do you remember? Are any of the postings true for your culture?

A Where were matchmakers used traditionally?

B I think it says in South Korea. It's interesting because my friend's mother had a matchmaker . . .

2 Grammar Adding information: time, place, possession

Figure it out

A Rewrite each pair of sentences as one sentence. Replace the words in bold with one word. Use the web page on page 116 to help you. Then read the grammar chart.

1. Things changed in the 1980s. **At that time**, people started to choose Western-style weddings.
2. After a wedding ceremony, the guests go to a reception. **There** they have a meal.
3. We used to use matchmakers. **Their** responsibility was to find the right husband or wife for you.

Relative clauses with *when*, *where*, and *whose*		*Grammar extra* *See page 164.*
When, *where*, and *whose* can introduce defining and non-defining relative clauses.		
Time – *when*	There's a touching moment **when** the bride walks down the aisle. The best time to get married is the summer, **when** it stays light all night.	
Place – *where*	There are places in the U.S. **where** a celebrity look-alike performs the ceremony. Some people go to Hawaii, **where** they get married on the beach.	
Possession – *whose*	I have lots of friends **whose** parents used a matchmaker. Some couples use a fortune-teller, **whose** job is to choose the best day.	

Common errors

Don't confuse *whose* with *who's* (= *who is* or *who has*).

About you

B Complete the postings with *when*, *where*, or *whose*. Often *when* and *where* are both correct. Then work with a partner. Compare traditions in your country with the ones below.

1. A week before the wedding, the bride and groom go to a photographer's studio, _____ the wedding photos are taken. The bride wears her wedding dress and everything.
2. Couples often marry at half past the hour, _____ the hands of the clock are moving up instead of down. It's believed that the marriage will get off to a good start.
3. After the bride and groom have exchanged rings, there's a ceremony _____ the bride and groom each light a candle.
4. At the reception, there's a dance _____ the guests pin money onto the bride's dress. There are some weddings _____ guests "pay" to dance with the bride or groom.
5. The best man, _____ job is to take care of the rings, also makes a speech at the reception.
6. My favorite part is the event _____ the bride is painted with henna. It's called the *Mehndi*.

3 Viewpoint Views on weddings

Group work Discuss the questions. Do you have similar experiences and views?

- Have you ever been to a wedding? If so, what kind of ceremony was it?
- Was it a traditional wedding, or was there something different about it?
- How important is it to keep wedding traditions?
- How much do people spend on average on weddings? Is it a waste of money?
- What's your idea of a perfect wedding?
- Which wedding traditions would you like to change?

In conversation . . .

You can repeat words or ask *Did you say . . .?* to show interest or surprise.

A I went to a wedding last year where the reception was at a theme park.
B A theme park? OR Did you say a theme park?

Unit 11: Culture **117**

Lesson B *Gift giving*

Grammar in context

A What gifts have you bought or given on the occasions below? On what other occasions do people give presents?

an engagement party   a retirement party   a housewarming party   a baby shower

B 🔊 CD 4.15 Listen and take the quiz. Check (✔) a, b, or c. If you check c, write your own answer.

Gift giving is an important part of every culture, but customs and attitudes can vary even within one culture. Take this quiz and then compare answers with a friend.

1 When someone gives me a gift, I usually . . .
- a) open it immediately.
- b) open it later when I'm alone.
- c) other _____

2 When someone gives me a present to open, I tend to . . .
- a) tear off the wrapping paper and throw it away.
- b) unwrap it carefully and save the paper.
- c) other _____

3 I give money or gift cards to friends on their birthdays . . .
- a) all the time or often.
- b) occasionally or very rarely.
- c) other _____

4 If someone bought me a gift that I didn't like, I would . . .
- a) "re-gift" it and give it to someone else.
- b) take it back to the store and exchange it.
- c) other _____

5 If a friend bought a birthday gift for my mother, . . .
- a) I'd buy something similar for his or her mother.
- b) I wouldn't buy his or her mother one in return.
- c) other _____

6 If a co-worker complimented me on something I was wearing (for example, jewelry), I'd . . .
- a) offer it to him or her as a gift.
- b) simply say "thank you."
- c) other _____

7 If a friend bought me a gift for my home and I hated it, I would . . .
- a) put it in a closet.
- b) feel obliged to display it.
- c) other _____

8 If a friend made a gift for me, I would . . .
- a) appreciate it more than a gift from a store.
- b) feel disappointed that it wasn't a real gift.
- c) other _____

About you | **C** Pair work Compare your answers. Do you share the same views?

A When someone gives me a gift, I open it immediately. It seems impolite to wait.

B I suppose. But if I get a gift before my birthday, I'll usually wait and open it on the day.

2 Grammar Giving things to people

Figure it out

A Complete the second sentence so it means the same as the first. Use the quiz to help you. Then read the grammar chart.

1. When someone gives a present to me, I open it. *When someone gives me* _____ .
2. I give my friends money or gift cards all the time. *I give money or gift cards* _____ .
3. If someone made me a gift, I'd love it. *If someone made a gift,* _____ .

Verbs with two objects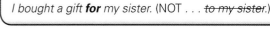

Grammar extra
See page 165.

Notice the patterns with verbs like *bring, buy, give, lend, make, offer, send.*

	indirect object	direct object		direct object	prepositional phrase
I never give	my friends / them	money.	I never give	money	**to** my friends / them.
She lent	someone	her book.	She lent	her book / it	**to** someone.
A friend sent	my mother	a gift.	A friend sent	a gift	**to** my mother.
I bought / made	his mother	something / one.	I bought / made	something / one	**for** his mother.

The pattern above is more common in general conversation, especially with *give*.

Use the pattern above when the direct object is *it* or *them*.

She lent **it** to **a friend.** (NOT ~~She lent a friend it.~~)

B Rewrite the questions using the alternate pattern in the chart. If it's not possible, write X.

Common errors

I bought a gift **for** my sister. (NOT . . . ~~to my sister.~~)

1. Would you ever buy a gift for your neighbor?   *Would you ever buy your neighbor a gift?*
2. When would you give a gift card to somebody?
3. When would you buy someone flowers? Would you give them to a teacher?
4. What would you think if someone sent you red roses out of the blue?
5. Imagine someone really liked a vase in your home. Would you offer it to that person?
6. Have you ever made someone a gift or a card? Did you make it for a friend?

About you

C Pair work Take turns asking and answering the questions. Give your own answers.

3 Listening and speaking Gift giving around the world

A What rules are there about these things in your culture? What do some gifts symbolize?

1. wrapping gifts   2. offering gifts   3. accepting gifts   4. inappropriate gifts

B ◀))CD 4.16 Listen to a radio interview about gift giving. What gifts are inappropriate in each country, according to the guest on the show? Write them in the chart. Then listen again and write the reason.

Country	Inappropriate gifts	Reason	Other advice
1. Japan			
2. Russia			
3. Chile			
4. Korea			
5. Mexico			

C ◀))CD 4.17 Listen to the rest of the interview. Write one more piece of advice for each country.

About you

D Pair work Prepare an interview on gift giving in your country.

"So, Fernando, when would you give flowers to someone in Brazil?"

Lesson C *It's kind of bizarre!*

 Conversation strategy Softening comments

A What do people do at birthday parties in your culture? What interesting traditions are there? Do people ever do bizarre things?

B 🔊 CD 4.18 Listen. What do Guy and Ann think about birthday traditions in different cultures?

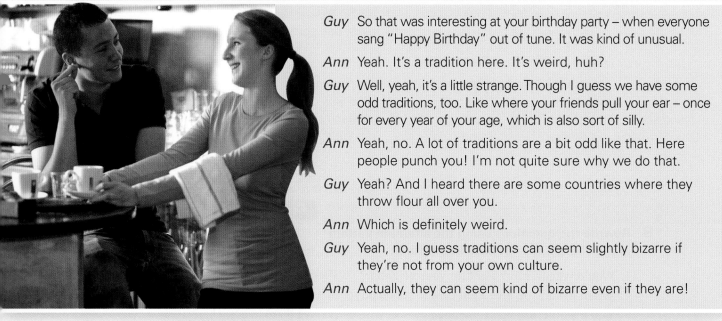

Guy So that was interesting at your birthday party – when everyone sang "Happy Birthday" out of tune. It was kind of unusual.

Ann Yeah. It's a tradition here. It's weird, huh?

Guy Well, yeah, it's a little strange. Though I guess we have some odd traditions, too. Like where your friends pull your ear – once for every year of your age, which is also sort of silly.

Ann Yeah, no. A lot of traditions are a bit odd like that. Here people punch you! I'm not quite sure why we do that.

Guy Yeah? And I heard there are some countries where they throw flour all over you.

Ann Which is definitely weird.

Guy Yeah, no. I guess traditions can seem slightly bizarre if they're not from your own culture.

Ann Actually, they can seem kind of bizarre even if they are!

C **Notice** how Guy and Ann soften their comments using expressions like these. Find examples in the conversation.

kind of	*a (little) bit*	*not really*
sort of	*slightly*	*not quite*
a little	*somewhat*	

In conversation . . .

Kind of, *a little*, and *sort of* are the most common expressions. *Somewhat* and *slightly* are more common in formal speaking. People often use *not quite* with *sure*, *right*, *true*, *clear*, and *certain*.

D 🔊 CD 4.19 Listen. Complete the conversations with the expressions you hear. Then practice with a partner. Practice again, this time giving your own responses.

1. *A* We have a tradition here where we put butter on kids' noses to avoid bad luck.
   B Which sounds _____ bizarre. I mean, it's _____ strange, huh?

2. *A* Here we turn people upside down and bang them on their head, which is crazy. I mean, it's _____ a good idea, is it?
   B No. It seems _____ dangerous to me. I mean, you could get hurt.

3. *A* On friends' birthdays, we used to pull their hair, which was _____ weird, I guess.
   B Yeah. It sounds _____ irritating. Well, _____ annoying, anyway.

4. *A* I think I'd be really upset if people threw flour all over me.
   B Me, too. It sounds _____ mean to me. It's _____ odd, anyway.

5. *A* At our kids' birthday parties, we throw them up in the air. I wonder why.
   B I'm _____ sure, but I guess it's _____ a fun thing to do!

② Strategy plus *Yeah, no.*

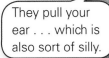

They pull your ear . . . which is also sort of silly.

Yeah, no. A lot of traditions are a bit odd like that.

◀)) CD 4.20 You can use *Yeah, no* to agree with someone and then make a comment of your own.

In conversation . . .

People almost always say *Yeah, no* rather than *Yes, no*.

A ◀))CD 4.21 **Listen to the start of five conversations. How does each one continue? Number the responses 1–5.**

_____ Yeah, no. It's good that people carry on traditions.
_____ Yeah, no. It's nice to do fun stuff with your friends on your birthday.
_____ Yeah, no. Society needs to recognize birthdays like 80 or 100.
_____ Yeah, no. It's good to celebrate special birthdays. Here it's when you're 18.
_____ Yeah, no. It's nice to celebrate with your family and have family memories.

About you **B** ◀))CD 4.22 **Pair work** **Listen and check. Then discuss each of the views in Exercise A. Do you agree?**

③ Strategies Funny family traditions

A **Complete the conversations. Add expressions to soften A's comments, and choose an appropriate response from the box. Then practice the conversations with a partner.**

| Kids can be kind of mean | It can be a little embarrassing. |
| It's bizarre how things like that get started. | Kids love fun things like that. |

1. *A* When my sister and I were little, my grandmother always gave us money on New Year's Day. But she didn't hand it to us. She put it in our shoes the night before, so we found it when we woke up the next morning. It was _____ unusual, but it was fun.
    B Yeah, no. _____

2. *A* We have a tradition on birthdays that's _____ silly, where we see who can buy the worst gift. It's _____ stupid, really, I guess. I'm _____ sure now why we do it.
    B Yeah, no. _____

3. *A* My family has a tradition of giving names to new babies by just picking places from a map, which is _____ bizarre! My sister wants to call her new baby Orinoco if it's a boy and Amazon if it's a girl. It's _____ unfair to the kids if you ask me.
    B Yeah, no. _____

4. *A* So every year on Halloween, we'd make this homemade candy with chili peppers in it. And we'd give it to friends like it was some nice gift. It was _____ mean, really.
    B Yeah, no. _____

About you **B** **Group work** **Think of two family traditions you have. Take turns telling the group about them. What are the most unusual traditions?**

"In my family, we have kind of a funny tradition on New Year's Day where we all have a big pillow fight. It's a little crazy, but it's always fun."

④ Speaking naturally Consonant groups *See page 143.*

Lesson D *Threats to culture*

1 Reading

A **Prepare** What things in your everyday life come from different cultures? Make a list.

"We get a lot of Chinese movies, and let's see, . . . there are lots of . . ."

B  **Read for main ideas** Read the article. What are some different aspects of culture? What can threaten culture?

Are we losing our culture?

¹ The word *culture* refers not only to the beliefs and customs of our society, to its art, literature, and music, but also to basic everyday activities, such as our eating habits, how we greet people, and how we dress. Cultures give us a sense of identity and belonging in society. Therefore, the loss of one's culture is, for many, alarming. In 46 out of 47 countries where opinion polls were taken, many people believe their traditional ways of life are under threat and that something should be done to ensure the preservation of their culture. Yet for some, the loss of culture is a natural result of globalization and progress, and an opportunity to embrace other cultures. So is the globalization of culture a threat or an opportunity?

² Those who see globalization as a threat argue that societies are losing unique aspects of their cultures. As an example, they cite the growing number of endangered languages, as English, Chinese, and Spanish, the main languages of business, spread globally. Omotik, a language spoken in East Africa, has only 50 surviving speakers. Consequently, it is in danger of extinction. There are also increasing fears in China, where the loss of musical and dance traditions, as well as traditional crafts, is causing concern to many.

³ Some who stress the downside of globalization complain that it is becoming increasingly difficult to distinguish Tokyo or Seoul from London or New York. The same chain restaurants and coffee shops exist worldwide, with identical logos and brands. Young people, whose ideas are often influenced by Western or other popular cultures, wear the same fashions, tend to watch the same movies, and adopt similar ideas – often neglecting or even rejecting the traditions their parents grew up with.

⁴ Others dismiss such concerns and instead focus on the benefits of globalization. They accept that Western culture is spreading, but they also point to how Western countries and many other parts of the world are being exposed to world cultures. Young Americans enjoy Japanese manga magazines and watch Korean movies. British youth are familiar with Brazilian martial arts. Thai teenagers download pop music from Hong Kong, while young French students take on internships in Shanghai. Many argue there are benefits to these cross-cultural exchanges and that they lead to better understanding between cultures. They say world traditions are celebrated more widely because of this. Chinese New Year, now celebrated in most big cities around the world, is just one of the many festivals that are recognized internationally.

⁵ Nevertheless, many grass-roots organizations and governments are making efforts to guarantee the protection of their cultures. One successful example is Wales. There was a time when social pressures were killing off the Welsh language, but after decades of effort, it is now a vibrant part of Welsh life again. Around the world, there are similar efforts to revive local languages, music, foods, crafts, and traditional sports. Ironically, it might well be that the threat of losing a culture will ultimately lead to its rejuvenation.

Reading tip

Those, many, some, and *others* often refer to groups of pe
*The loss of one's culture is, for **many**, alarming.*
(= for many people)

C Understanding viewpoints Would the writer of the article agree (A) or disagree (D) with the statements below? Write A or D.

1. Many people say they are worried about threats to culture. ____
2. Most big cities are unique and have their own identity. ____
3. English is the only business language. ____
4. Increasingly, young people are continuing the traditions of their parents. ____
5. Young people are rarely exposed to cross-cultural exchanges. ____
6. Many festivals that were once local now take place around the world. ____

About you | **D** React Pair work Are the sentences in Exercise C true for your society? Discuss.

"I think people worry about losing our culture. You rarely hear traditional music anymore."

② Focus on vocabulary Opposites

A Find words in the article that are opposite in meaning to the words in bold. Paragraph numbers where you can find the words are in parentheses. Use the words to complete the questions below.

1. What do you think about the **loss** of culture? Is the <u>preservation</u> of culture important? (para. 1)
2. In what ways is globalization a **threat**? In what ways is it an _____? (para. 1)
3. What is the **downside** of global brands and chain restaurants? What are the _____? (para. 4)
4. Why do some _____ the view that loss of culture is bad, even though others **accept** it? (para. 4)
5. Is modern life **killing off** any traditions in your culture? Which could you _____? (para. 5)
6. What are some of the _____ traditions in your area? What **global** celebrations are observed? (para. 5)

B Pair work Discuss the questions in Exercise A. Do you have the same views?

"I think the loss of culture matters. Countries where culture is under threat will lose their identity."

③ Listening and speaking Reviving a dying language

About you | **A** 🔊 CD 4.25 Read the list of things that can be done to revive a dying language. Add other ideas. Then listen to a seminar discussion. Check (✔) the ideas the students discuss.

☐ teach it in elementary school   ☐ translate public signs and notices
☐ make it mandatory in college   ☐ pay higher salaries to people who speak it
☐ offer homestays in areas where it's spoken   ☐ use it on TV and radio, and in other media

About you | **B** 🔊 CD 4.26 Listen again. Underline the two ideas that the students agree might work.

C 🔊 CD 4.27 The students repeat some of the ideas in the article on page 122, but use different forms of the words. Listen again and write the missing words.

1. Is language <u>revival</u> possible? (revive)
2. A language may become _____ . (extinction)
3. We need to _____ our culture, too. (preservation)
4. Can this _____ to a language help? (exposed)
5. The _____ of English is inevitable. (growing)
6. Globalization _____ languages. (threat)

About you | **D** Group work Discuss the advantages and disadvantages of the various ways to revive a language. Agree on the best three ways. Can they help with learning English?

Writing *Are we losing it?*

In this lesson, you . . .
- structure a conclusion.
- explain cause and effect with *due to*, etc.
- avoid errors with *due to*.

Task   Write a conclusion to an essay.

Are we in danger of losing our culture as a result of globalization?

A   Look at the models Read the thesis statements and the two concluding paragraphs below. Which statement appeared in the introduction to each essay? Write a, b, or c above each paragraph. There is one extra option.

a. It is not possible to tell if our culture is in danger, **because** it is too early. Only history will tell us.

b. In this essay, I will argue that we are in danger of losing our culture **as a result of** globalization.

c. In my view, it is **because of** globalization that we have opportunities to learn about other cultures.

Concluding paragraphs in an essay . . .
- restate the thesis statement.
- summarize the arguments.
- give a clear opinion.
- can start with *In summary* or *In conclusion*.

1. _____
In conclusion, our culture is in danger **due to** globalization. We may not be able to preserve it **because** people are attracted by new ideas and ways of life. **Consequently**, we should take action now to show young people the value of our unique culture and encourage them to preserve it.

2. _____
In summary, there are clearly positive and negative effects of globalization. However, it is difficult to know if it will damage our culture. **Therefore**, we need to wait for the judgment of future generations **since** they will be in a better position to see its impact.

B   Focus on language The bold expressions in Exercise A link causes with effects or results. Circle the causes. Then read the grammar chart.

Expressing cause and effect in writing

	EFFECT	CAUSE
Use *as a result of, because of,* and *due to* + a noun.	*Our culture is in danger* **due to** *globalization.*	
Use *because* or *since* + a clause.		**since** *we are attracted by new ideas.*

	CAUSE	EFFECT/RESULT
Therefore and *Consequently* often start sentences.	*Our culture is in danger.*	**Consequently**, *we should take action.*
Use *so* mid-sentence.	*Our culture is in danger,*	**so** *we should take action.*

C   Complete the concluding paragraphs below with expressions from the chart.

1. In conclusion, our culture has changed _____ globalization has brought us many new ideas and customs. These ideas are attractive, _____ they are replacing some of our traditions. _____ , we are in danger of losing our traditional values.

2. In summary, cultures are constantly changing _____ migration, trade, and tourism. We learn more about the world _____ we are exposed to new people and ideas. _____ , we should see globalization as positive.

D   Write and check Write a concluding paragraph that gives your answer to the question in the Task above. Include two arguments to support your answer. Then check for errors.

Common errors

Use *due to* to give causes. Avoid using *due to* to say why people do things. Use *because (of)*.

Vocabulary notebook *Wedding bells!*

Learning tip   Word webs

You can write new vocabulary in word webs. Word webs are useful for writing down vocabulary about a topic. They can be as simple or as complex as you wish.

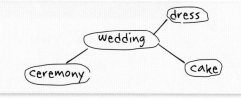

A   Complete the word web with the words in the box. Then add other vocabulary from page 116.

arranged marriage	best man	bride	civil ceremony	✓ groom

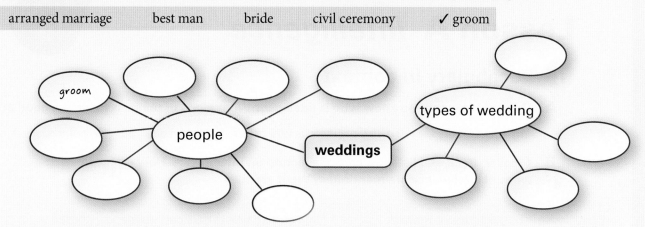

B   Now make your own word web for things people do at a wedding. Choose one more topic (for example, things people wear, eat, or say), and add other vocabulary you know.

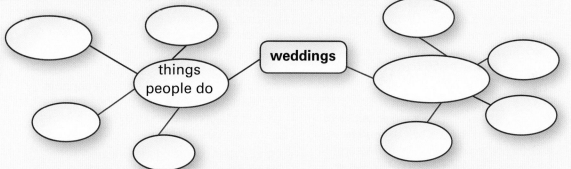

C   Word builder   Find the meanings of these expressions. Then add them to a word web.

a bouquet	a veil	a wedding planner	to go on (a, your) honeymoon	to throw rice or confetti
a maid of honor	a wedding band	a wedding registry	to propose (to someone)	

On your own

Write a blog about a wedding you have been to or know about. Highlight key words and expressions. Find photos to illustrate the blog.

What goes with *weddings*?

Here are the top ten words people use with the word *wedding* in writing and conversation: *wedding . . . present(s), anniversary, dress, ring(s), band(s), cake, gift(s), reception, vows, ceremony.*

Deepak and Amrita got married on May 21. It was a traditional Indian ceremony.

12 Ability

In Unit 12, you . . .

- talk about intelligence, skills, and abilities.
- use adverbs and adjectives to describe and compare.
- use vague expressions when you don't need to be precise.
- agree with someone using responses like *No doubt*.

Lesson A *Intelligence*

1 Vocabulary in context

A Think of someone you know who is intelligent. What kinds of things is he or she good at?

"My friend Ahmed, who's a civil engineer, is very intelligent. He's good at designing things."

B 🔊 CD 4.28 Read and listen to part of a lecture on intelligence. How many different types of intelligence are mentioned? What are they?

1 "Today I'll be talking about Howard Gardner, the highly respected professor of psychology at Harvard University. His work has been particularly important in terms of its impact on education. Gardner argues that defining intelligence as one single thing is both imprecise and inadequate, and suggests instead that there are different types of intelligences.

2 The first is **linguistic** intelligence. People who are linguistically intelligent **are sensitive to** language. They're extremely **articulate** and **literate** and may become writers, actors, or lawyers. They're often highly **skilled at** learning languages, too.

3 The second is **logical-mathematical** intelligence. These people **are scientifically minded** and **have a capacity for** investigating things. They're especially good at math and **are efficient at** solving problems – often incredibly quickly.

4 The third type is **musical** intelligence – those who **have a talent for** music. And the fourth is **bodily** intelligence. People with this **are able to** learn through movement; they use their bodies effectively – for example, they can balance relatively easily, like dancers or gymnasts.

5 The fifth intelligence is **spatial** intelligence. People with this **are capable of** creating drawings and designs that are technically correct, and may be architects and designers.

6 Other types of intelligence include **interpersonal** and **intrapersonal** intelligence. People with interpersonal intelligence **are** particularly **adept at** understanding others, while those with intrapersonal intelligence are remarkably good at understanding themselves.

7 These seven types make up Gardner's original theory. He later added . . ."

Word sort

C Make a chart like the one below for each type of intelligence. Use the words and expressions in bold from the lecture. Then complete the chart with your own ideas.

Type of intelligence	People with it . . .	They would make good . . .
linguistic	are articulate	writers, actors, lawyers, teachers

Vocabulary notebook
See page 135.

About you

D Pair work Rate yourselves on a scale of 1–10 for each type of intelligence (1 = very bad at; 10 = very good at). Discuss your ideas.

"I'd say I'm good at languages and pretty articulate, so I'd give myself a 7 for linguistic intelligence."

2 Grammar Describing people and things

Figure
it out

A How does the lecturer express the ideas in bold? Use the lecture to help you rewrite the sentences. Then read the grammar chart.

1. Some people are **very skilled** at learning languages.
2. These people **have scientific minds**.
3. Some people solve problems **quickly – I think it's incredible**.
4. These people are **adept at one thing that I want to focus on – they understand others**.

Adverbs

Grammar extra
See page 166.

You can use adverbs like these before adjectives and adverbs to introduce these ideas.

Degree – e.g., *extremely, highly, relatively*	They're **extremely** literate and **highly** skilled.
Type – e.g., *scientifically, linguistically*	**Linguistically** intelligent people are good at languages.
Opinion – e.g., *incredibly, remarkably*	They seem to solve problems **incredibly** easily.
Focus – e.g., *especially, particularly*	People with logical intelligence are **especially** good at math.

Common errors

Don't use an adjective to describe an adjective. *I'm very **physically active**.* (NOT . . . ~~physical active~~)

About
you

B Unscramble the words to make questions. Then ask and answer the questions with a partner.

Do you know anyone who . . .

1. especially directions giving good at is?
2. well communicates with extremely other people?
3. is in interested himself or herself particularly?
4. any sports incapable of playing is completely?
5. clearly remarkably his or her ideas articulates?
6. quickly incredibly does mental math?
7. highly is maps drawing skilled at?
8. talented is musically?
9. well fairly chess plays?
10. easily languages relatively learns?

3 Listening and speaking Minds for the future

A Match the two parts of each sentence below. What are the five "minds" good at?

☐ A synthesizing mind
☐ An ethical mind
☐ A disciplined mind
☐ A respectful mind
☐ A creative mind

a. focuses particularly well on doing what is right.
b. works extremely hard.
c. takes other people's views and feelings very seriously.
d. is very adept at thinking in new and different ways.
e. can sort through facts to decide what is relevant.

Professor Howard Gardner

B 🔊 CD 4.29 Listen. José is telling Olga about an article on the five minds by Howard Gardner. Number 1–5 the five minds in Exercise A in the order he talks about them.

C 🔊 CD 4.29 Listen again. Circle the minds that Olga says she has.

About
you

D Group work Which of the five minds do you have? Which do you still need to work on? How could schools and universities help students to develop in these five areas?

"I think I have a disciplined mind. I mean, I tend to work extremely hard and . . ."

4 Speaking naturally Stress and intonation See page 143.

Lesson B *Improving skills*

1 Grammar in context

A What unusual or interesting skills do you have? How good are you at each of them? Make a class list.

"Actually, I'm an extremely fast reader. I learned how to speed-read in high school."

B 🔊 CD 4.32 Listen to the interviews. What skill has each person improved? How?

Have you improved any of your skills in the last year?

Linda Ho

"Actually, one thing I've gotten better at is speaking in public. I used to hate doing presentations at work – it was the worst thing. And you know, the more I thought about it, the worse I'd feel. I'd just get so nervous. But then I took a public-speaking course – it seemed the best and most sensible thing to do. And that helped, so, yeah, I definitely feel happier now. I'm more confident and less nervous than I used to be, which is good."

Nurdan Ozdag

"I took up the flute a year or so ago, and I *am* improving, . . . more slowly than I'd hoped, but hey – it's not an easy instrument. It's like anything, the harder you practice, the better you get. I probably don't play as often as I should. It's hard to find time with my job – work just gets busier and busier."

Bryan Jarvis

"I started mountain biking a few years back, and I just got really into it and decided to race competitively. It was actually much more difficult than I thought it would be. My biggest challenge will be a 50K* race next year. It'll be the furthest I've ever cycled. I've been training harder than ever – most often on weekends – so I'm cycling faster. I'm not as fast as I'd like to be, but I'm doing better."

(*50 kilometers or approximately 31 miles)

C Pair work Answer the questions about the interviews. Check (✔) the names.

Who . . .	Linda	Nurdan	Bryan
do you think has made the most progress?			
would benefit from more practice?			
had a fear of doing something?			
is most serious about improving his or her skills?			
got help to improve?			

2 Grammar Comparing

Figure it out

A How do the people in the interviews express the ideas below? Write the sentences they used. Then read the grammar chart.

1. Linda: I definitely feel happy now – I didn't before.
2. Nurdan: I *am* improving, but it's slower than I'd hoped.
3. Nurdan: I don't play very often. I should, though.
4. Bryan: I've never cycled further than this.

Comparative and superlative adjectives and adverbs

Grammar extra
See page 167.

	Comparatives and *as . . . as*	Superlatives
Adjectives	I feel **happier**, and I've gotten **better** at it. I'm **more confident** and **less nervous**. I'm not **as fast as** I'd like to be.	The race is my **biggest** and **best** challenge. Taking a course was **the most sensible** idea. I was **the least experienced** presenter.
Adverbs	I'm training **harder** than ever. I'm improving **more slowly** than I'd hoped. I practice **less often** than I should. I don't play **as often as** I should.	We all train hard, but I train **(the) hardest**. I train **(the) most often** on weekends. (Superlative adverbs with *least* are not common.)

Common errors

Use *in* for places and organizations. *I'm the fastest rider **in** the club.* (NOT . . . *of the club.*)
Don't confuse *worse* and *worst*. *The **worst** thing is speaking . . .* (NOT *The worse thing . . .*)

About you

B ◀ CD 4.33 Circle the correct words to complete the conversations. Then listen and check. Practice the conversations with a partner, giving your own answers.

1. *A* What do you do **better** / **well** now than a couple of years ago?
   B Well, I feel more **confidently** / **confident** about math. I'm better **that** / **than** I was. I'm not the best **in** / **of** my class, but I can do the problems **easy** / **more easily** now.

2. *A* Of all your skills, what do you do **better** / **the best**?
   B I'm a pretty good photographer. Though I don't take photos as **much** / **frequent** as I'd like.
   A Yeah? I'm the **worse** / **worst** photographer in the world.

3. *A* Are you good at sports? I mean, are you as good **as** / **than** you'd like to be?
   B I like baseball, but it's getting **harder** / **hardest** to find time to play.

4. *A* What's the **harder** / **hardest** thing you ever tried to learn to do?
   B Pottery. It looks **easier** / **more easily** than it is. But if you practice, you get **the best** / **better**.

3 Viewpoint I'm getting better and better . . .

Pair work Discuss the questions below and ask questions of your own. Then prepare a one-minute presentation about your partner to give to the class.

- Think of a skill you have. When did you start learning it?
- How did you learn the skill? Was it harder than you imagined?
- How long did it take to improve? How much better did you get?
- What advice do you have for someone who's improving a skill?

In conversation . . .

You can respond with *I bet* to show you understand what someone is talking about.

A Well, one skill I've been working on is drawing cartoons. I'm getting better, but it's hard.
B I bet. How did you get interested in it?

Lesson C . . . and all that.

1 Conversation strategy Using vague expressions

A **Think of talented famous people. How are (or were) they gifted?**

"Lang Lang is extremely talented. He started playing the piano at the age of three."

B 🔊 CD 4.34 **Listen. What examples of talent do Jenna and Sam talk about?**

Jenna Did you see that movie about that kid? She was three years old, and she did all these paintings and things and sold them for thousands of dollars.

Sam Yeah, I heard about that. Unbelievable, huh?

Jenna I mean, do you *learn* to paint and draw and stuff? Or are you just born with that kind of talent?

Sam Good question. It's the nature versus nurture thing. Her parents were probably always pushing her and everything.

Jenna It's like those six-year-old pianists that play classical concerts and that kind of thing. You have to be gifted.

Sam No doubt. But I'm sure they still have to do a lot of hard work and practice and all that.

Jenna True. But I still can't do paintings and that kind of thing.

Sam I know. Me neither. It's too bad when a six-year-old is more talented than you!

C **Notice** how Sam and Jenna use vague expressions like these. They don't need to be precise because the other person knows what they mean. Find the expressions they use in the conversation.

> . . . *and things (like that) / and stuff (like that)*
> . . . *and all / and all that*
> . . . *and that kind of thing / and that sort of thing*
> . . . *and everything*

In conversation . . .

Many vague expressions are less common in formal speaking. A more formal vague expression is *and so on*.

	Formal speaking	Conversation
and so on		
and all that		
and things		
and stuff		

About you

D **What do you think the expressions in bold mean? Write an idea for each one. Then compare with a partner. Do you agree with the statements?**

— or born with talent

1. Anyone can play an instrument or learn a language. You don't have to be gifted **and all that**.
2. I think you can be good at most things – if you practice **and everything**.
3. I don't think artists just learn to draw **and stuff**. I think they're born with a talent for it.
4. I can't stand it when parents make their kids perform on stage **and that kind of thing**.
5. I think if parents push their kids **and that sort of thing**, the kids usually end up hating it.
6. I think anyone can learn to do practical jobs, like fix their own cars **and things like that**.

"I'm not sure. I think you have to have a special talent for music and things like that."

2 Strategy plus *No doubt.*

You have to be gifted.

No doubt.

🔊 CD 4.35 You can say *No doubt* to show that you strongly agree with someone.

In conversation . . .

(No) doubt is also used in these related expressions.
There's no doubt about it / that. ■■■■■■■■■
Without a doubt. ■■■
I don't doubt it. ■

A 🔊 CD 4.36 **Listen to things five people say. Choose the correct responses and number them 1–5.**

_____ I don't doubt it. I think it helps you learn languages, too.

_____ No doubt. They get all that pressure and everything.

_____ Oh, no doubt. Performing in public can be very scary.

_____ Oh, without a doubt. If you don't like doing something, you can't do it well.

_____ Oh, no doubt about it. My friend plays the piano remarkably well, and she never learned it formally.

B 🔊 CD 4.37 **Now listen to the full conversations and check. Do you agree with the views?**

3 Listening and strategies The genius in all of us

A 🔊 CD 4.38 **Listen to a radio show. According to the show, are the sentences true (T) or false (F)? Write T or F.**

1. The writer David Shenk thinks people are born with certain talents. _____

2. London cab drivers' brains are generally bigger than most people's. _____

3. Your home and school are the most important influences for developing a skill. _____

4. The composer Mozart was successful because he was taught by his father. _____

5. The basketball player Michael Jordan trained with players who were better than him. _____

B 🔊 CD 4.39 **Listen to the conversations below about the radio show. Complete each one with the expressions you hear. Then practice with a partner.**

1. **A** Do you believe we're born with talent, or do we develop it through practice?
   B Hmm. Probably both. I mean, if you're a natural athlete, you won't become *really* good if your parents and teachers don't encourage you _____ .
   A _____ . Yeah. It's the same for music _____ .

2. **A** Do you think children can succeed at anything if they're encouraged more?
   B _____ . My teacher gave me extra books to read _____ . I'm sure that helped me with my studies _____ .

3. **A** Do you think some parents push their kids too hard?
   B Yeah. My mom made my sister take ballet _____ . She hated it. It was a waste of money.
   A _____ . I mean, swimming and _____ are useful, but . . .

About you

C **Class survey** **Ask your classmates the questions in Exercise B. Then prepare a short report to give to the class. What do your classmates say about talent?**

Lesson D Ability, not disability

 **Reading**

A Prepare Look at the photos and the title of the article. Can you guess what the article is about?

B 📥 **Read for main ideas** Read the exclusive interview with Chris Waddell. What are some of Chris's achievements?

Seeing things in a *completely* different way . . .

1   After sitting and talking with Chris Waddell for 20 minutes, you feel like anything is possible. Not so remarkable, perhaps, since he is a world-champion skier, and he has also climbed Mount Kilimanjaro – if it were not for the fact that Chris is sitting in a wheelchair and is paralyzed from the waist down. The ski accident that caused his paralysis happened when Chris was a college student. Nevertheless, just two years after his accident, he won a place on the U.S. Adaptive Ski Team. During the next 11 years, he won a total of 12 ski medals and, as a result, became the most decorated male skier in Paralympic history.

2   But Chris is not one to rest on past achievements. His mission to climb Mount Kilimanjaro, the highest mountain in Africa, was just another of the ways Chris is proving that we should change the way in which we view people with special needs. This is why I visited him at his Utah base – so that I could learn more about this incredibly difficult challenge and what inspired it.

3   **Q: So, Chris, what does being disabled actually mean to you? What is it that motivates you?**
A: I look at it this way. We all have certain shortcomings. It's just that some are more visible than others. I think I'm extremely fortunate. Through my disability, I've done things and met people – presidents even – that I would never have met otherwise.

4   **Q: What inspired the climb up Mount Kilimanjaro?**
A: Well, the date I chose to climb Mount Kilimanjaro was a halfway point in my life. I'd spent half of my life in a wheelchair. So it was a personal challenge – I am first and foremost an athlete – but I did it also in order to shine a light back on the disabled. To show that if you take the time to look, you might be surprised. People generally have a lot of preconceived ideas about disabled people. I wanted my climb to challenge those views, and so that people would start to see the 21-plus million disabled people in the world in a completely different light. It's about raising awareness.

5   **Q: How did you actually achieve it?**
A: I chose Mount Kilimanjaro because it's more readily accessible. You don't need ice picks and so on. But I used a specially adapted bicycle that I push with my arms. It was very physically challenging, and it took every last bit of my  strength, but I had a team of friends, a doctor, and porters, who carried the supplies. Also a film crew, who made the documentary about the climb.

6   Chris Waddell has dedicated his life to defying the conventional wisdom of what a paraplegic can and cannot do. As a result, he has become a role model for all of us.

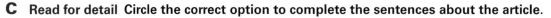
Visit Chris's website and be inspired!

C Read for detail Circle the correct option to complete the sentences about the article.

1. Before his accident, Chris Waddell was **a ski champion / a climber / a student**.
2. Compared to other male Paralympic skiers, he won **more / fewer / as many** medals.
3. Climbing Mount Kilimanjaro was an attempt to change **attitudes / his career / history**.
4. He chose Mount Kilimanjaro because it was **the most difficult / the closest / possible to climb**.
5. Chris found the climb **difficult / easy / not very challenging**.

D Paraphrase **Complete the paragraph with the expressions in the box.**

completely different	physically challenging	special needs
extremely fortunate	readily accessible	specially adapted

One of the things Chris believes is that everyone should see people with _____ and disabilities in a _____ way. He feels he has been _____ to have the chances he's had. But in reality, Chris has created his own opportunities. In order to highlight his cause, he has taken on a series of _____ projects. Although Mount Kilimanjaro is _____ to many people, Chris used a _____ bicycle so that he could complete the climb. Chris proved yet again that anything is possible!

② Focus on vocabulary Collocations

A **Find words in the article that are used with the words in bold. Use the words to complete the sentences below.**

1. Chris is a _____-_____ **skier**. He's at the top of his sport. (para. 1)
2. He has _____ half his **life** paralyzed. (para. 4)
3. Chris hopes that his achievements will _____ a light on people with special needs. (para. 4)
4. People often **have** _____ **ideas** about being disabled and don't know what it means. (para. 4)
5. Chris likes to _____ people's **views** and make them think. (para. 4)
6. His mission in life is _____ **awareness** about disabilities. (para. 4)
7. He has _____ his **life** to showing what people like him can do. (para. 6)
8. _____ **wisdom** says people like Chris can't climb a mountain. How wrong is that? (para. 6)

B Pair work **Take turns using the expressions in Exercise A to retell Chris's story. Which of his achievements do you find the most impressive?**

"Chris became a world-champion skier after his accident. It's incredible that he did that."

③ Viewpoint Disability and the community

Group work **Discuss the questions. Can you agree on one action point for the last two questions?**

- Do you know of any people who have overcome a disability to achieve something? How did they manage to do this?
- Do you personally know people who live with disabilities? What difficulties – if any – do they face?
- What views do people generally have of disabled people? Do any of these views need to be challenged?
- What facilities are there for people with special needs? What else could be provided?
- What do you think could be done to provide more opportunities for disabled people?

"One of our neighbors has Down Syndrome, and she's the most amazing athlete. She's incredibly motivated."

> **In conversation . . .**
> You can use a superlative adjective to make a description of someone or something stronger.

Writing *Extraordinary achievements*

In this lesson, you . . .
- brainstorm, then structure an essay.
- explain purpose with *so (that)*, etc.
- avoid errors with *so that*.

Task   Write an essay.

Choose a person that you admire and say why you admire the person. Use specific reasons and details to support your answer.

A   **Look at a model** Read part of an essay. Why did Gladys: a) leave home? b) go back to college? c) retire early? Circle the expressions the writer uses to introduce Gladys's purpose in doing things.

> One person that I admire is my mother, Gladys, because of her passion for life and for helping people. She left home at the age of 16 (so that) she could train as a nurse and then a midwife. After starting a family, she went back to college in order to qualify as a midwifery teacher. She suffered a serious illness in her fifties so she retired early to regain her health. Then, at the age of 69, she decided to enter local politics in order to give something back to her community. She ran for election and won a seat on the city council, where she worked tirelessly to help local citizens. Seven years later, she became mayor of the city.
>
> Her passion for life was evident at a young age. Leaving home was a big adventure for a teenage girl from a small village. She . . .

B   **Focus on language** Read the grammar chart. Then complete the sentences below, using alternate expressions from the model.

Explaining purpose in writing

You can use *so (that)* + clause or *(in order) to* + verb to describe purpose.
*She left home at the age of 16 **so (that)** she could train as a nurse.*
*She went back to college **(in order) to** qualify as a midwifery teacher.*

Common errors

Use *so* or *so that* to introduce a purpose. Use *so* but not *so that* to introduce a result or an effect.
*She suffered a serious illness, **so** she retired early.* (NOT . . . ~~so that she retired early.~~)

1. Gladys left school at the age of 16 _in order to train as a nurse_ .
2. She went back to college _____ .
3. She retired early _____ .
4. She decided to enter local politics _____ .

C   **Brainstorm and plan** Brainstorm ideas for your essay, using the points below. Then use the model to plan your essay.

- Choose a person you admire.
- Say why you admire him or her.
- Give examples of things he or she did and why.

Introduction	→	Include a thesis statement.
Supporting paragraphs	→	Write a topic sentence and supporting sentences with examples, reasons, arguments.
Conclusion	→	Restate the thesis statement.

D   **Write and check** Now write your essay. Then check for errors.

Vocabulary notebook *It's just the opposite!*

A   Write the opposites of the words below. Use the prefixes *il, in,* or *un.*

1. articulate ≠ _inarticulate_

2. sensitive ≠ _____

3. literate ≠ _____

4. skilled ≠ _____

5. efficient ≠ _____

6. able ≠ _____

7. capable ≠ _____

8. important ≠ _____

9. correct ≠ _____

10. complete ≠ _____

B   Now write opposites for these expressions.

1. be adept at ≠ _____

2. be bad at ≠ _____

3. have a capacity for ≠ _____

4. have a talent for ≠ _____

C   Word builder Find and write the opposites of these adjectives. Use *il-, im-, in-, ir-,* or *un-.*

1. adequate
≠ _____

2. effective
≠ _____

3. convenient
≠ _____

4. legal
≠ _____

5. logical
≠ _____

6. likely
≠ _____

7. necessary
≠ _____

8. patient
≠ _____

9. precise
≠ _____

10. relevant
≠ _____

On your own

Make a word game. Write pairs of cards – one with a word
and one with a prefix that can be used with that word.
Then play a game with a friend. Shuffle the cards and
place them face up. Take turns picking out matching cards.

im   in   un   precise   likely   il   literate   correct

Checkpoint 4 *Units 10–12*

 It's not as difficult as . . .

A How many words and expressions can you think of to describe weddings?

1. Western-style wedding

B Complete the TV interviews with the comparative or superlative form of the words given. Some use *less* or *least,* and some need *than.* Use *as . . . as* with the underlined words.

"In many countries, people are getting married _____ (late) in life. Many young people are thinking about marriage _____ (carefully), and some are not marrying at all. But why? Our reporter, Dan Browning, interviewed a bride at her wedding."

1. **Dan** Why did you decide to get married in your forties? Do you feel _____ (confident) you did when you were _____ (young)?

   Lisa Well, getting married was _____ (big) decision I've ever made – and obviously it's _____ (important). I waited because I was working _____ (hard) I could on my career. I might not have been _____ (successful) I am if I had gotten married _____ (early).

2. **Dan** Tell me, is staying single _____ (difficult) it used to be?

   Lisa I don't think so. People generally don't feel _____ (pressured) they used to to get married. It's _____ (good) to take your time. When I was young, I was _____ (sure) I am right now about life. My advice for young people is "Enjoy life and don't rush into marriage."

3. **Dan** Can you tell me: How much have you spent on your wedding?

   Lisa We're not sure. But we chose everything _____ (carefully) we could to keep the costs down. We even bought the _____ (expensive) dress we could find. But still, we'll be paying for the wedding for years! I guess we'll worry about that tomorrow.

C Report the interview in Exercise B, using the verbs *ask, explain, tell,* and *say* as in the sentence stems below. Sometimes there is more than one correct answer.

> The interviewer asked . . .   She explained . . .   She told him . . .   She also said . . .

The interviewer asked Lisa why she had decided to get married in her forties. She explained . . .

About you

D **Pair work** Discuss the interview in Exercise B. Use expressions with *no doubt* when you agree. Use expressions like *so what you're saying is* to draw conclusions.

A I think a lot of people are waiting longer before they get married.
B There's no doubt. OR So, what you're saying is people are older when they get married?

That's talent!

A Rewrite the sentences. Write complete expressions with the words in parentheses. Add words from the box. Rewrite the underlined sentences in a different way, if possible.

articulate	✓ interpersonal	literate	logical	musical	sensitive

has a capacity for

1. My sister (capacity) understanding others. You know, she has great interpersonal skills. She's very _____ to people's feelings and everything. <u>She always gives good advice to me.</u>

   She always gives me good advice.

2. My best friend is very _____ . She (able) pick up any instrument and play it. <u>A friend once lent her a guitar. She was playing it within three weeks!</u>

3. I love to talk, and I'm pretty _____ . I (pretty skilled) learning languages, too. <u>My parents bought me some Italian-language CDs when I was a kid. I listened to them all the time.</u>

4. <u>I sent my niece some calligraphy pens for her birthday.</u> She (talent) drawing and all that.

5. My sister (really good) singing and dancing. <u>She made a recording of her last show for us. My mom sent it to everyone!</u>

6. My brother has always read a lot since he was little. He's very _____ . You know he's very smart and he (capable) doing anything, really.

7. My dad (so efficient) solving problems and things. <u>I gave my math homework to him last week. He did it in 20 minutes.</u> He's just very _____ , I guess.

B **Pair work** Use the ideas in Exercise A to talk about people you know. Use *In what way?* to ask for details. Use expressions like *and all that* when you don't need to be precise.

A *My English teacher has really good interpersonal skills and stuff.*
B *Yeah? In what way?*

3 Traveling

A Rewrite the conversations. Use the correct adverb and adjective forms of the words in parentheses. Rewrite the underlined sentences as one sentence using *when, where,* or *whose.*

1. *A* What's the most (physical / challenge) thing you've ever done?
   B Well, the trek to Machu Picchu was kind of (exhaust). But it was worth it because it is an (incredible / impress) place. My friend did the climb (relative / easy), which was a little (depress) because he's ten years older than me. He was fine, but I was (total / exhaust) by the time we got there. But <u>I remember the first morning there. We got up early and watched the sunrise.</u> That was just (amaze).

   A *What's the most physically challenging thing you've ever done?*

2. *A* What's the most (frighten) thing you've ever done?
   B I'm not really sure. Maybe going on a roller coaster on my birthday. I was (absolutely / terrify). <u>There's a really great amusement park near here. Young people go to celebrate birthdays.</u> Anyway, I started off (complete / relax). <u>I was sort of OK, till we got to the top. I looked down and started screaming.</u> It was windy that day, so it was (particular / terrify).

B **Pair work** Take turns asking and answering the questions in Exercise A. Use softening comments if necessary. Use *Yeah, no* to agree and then make a comment of your own.

A *I helped my friend move here last week, and that was kind of exhausting.*
B *Yeah, no. Moving is unbelievably tiring.*

Unit 7, Lesson C Conversational expressions

Notice how the speakers say the bold expressions quickly, in one breath.

■

What I'm saying is, most young people can't afford to live on their own.

■

To be honest, it's almost impossible to buy your own place.

A ◀))) CD 3.10 Read and listen to the information above. Repeat the example sentences.

B ◀))) CD 3.11 Listen and repeat. Say the expressions in bold as quickly as you can.

1. I like living with my parents. **I'm not saying** I won't move out one day. But for now it's fine.
2. **To be honest with you**, I feel sorry for people who live alone. **What I mean is**, they must get lonely sometimes. **I have to say,** I'd hate it.
3. **To tell you the truth**, it's hard to live far away from your relatives. **What I'm saying is**, it's just good to be near family. **I mean**, it just feels better somehow.
4. You can't do much about it if you don't like your college roommate. **In other words**, you're stuck.

About you   **C** Pair work Discuss the views in Exercise B. Which ones do you agree with?

Unit 8, Lesson C Strong and weak forms of prepositions

Notice how the speakers use strong forms of the prepositions *as, at, for, from, of,* and *to* at the end of a sentence. They use weak or reduced forms of these words in the middle of a sentence. However, *to* is strong before a word that starts with a vowel sound.

Strong forms	Weak forms
*"Some foods make vague claims." "Such **as**?"*	*"Claims such **as** 'improves digestion.'"*
*On a menu, what's the first thing you look **at**?*	*I look **at** the desserts first.*
*If you read food labels, what do you look **for**?*	*I look **for** additives – **for** instance, food coloring.*
*Where do you get Vitamin D **from**?*	*You can get it **from** the sun.*
*What's chewing gum made **of**?*	*It's often made **of** gum, sugar, and flavors.*
*What do they add sugar **to**? **To** all foods?*	*It's added **to** lots of foods, like cereals and . . .*

A ◀))) CD 3.21 Read and listen to the information above. Repeat the example sentences.

B ◀))) CD 3.22 Listen. Circle the strong forms of the prepositions. Draw a line (/) through the weak forms. Then practice with a partner.

1. *A* What foods can you get Vitamin C (from)? I mean, what foods should I look **for**?
   B Well, you can get it **from** vegetables such **as** broccoli and bell peppers.
   A So, do you think getting a lot **of** Vitamin C stops you **from** getting colds?
   B I'm not sure, but it is added **to** lots **of** foods.

2. *A* Which foods contain fat?
   B I'm not sure. I know some processed foods are full **of** it.
   A Such **as**?
   B Well, processed cheese, **for** example. Which is sad, because I eat a lot **of** cheese.

3. *A* What foods do manufacturers add sugar **to**? And what do they add it **for**?
   B Oh, they add it **to** almost everything – **from** soups **to** cereals. I mean, you need to look **at** the label to find out. That's what I always look **at**. Look out **for** corn syrup, too. That's a kind **of** sugar. People have gotten used to the taste, I guess.

4 Unit 9, Lesson C Stress in expressions

Notice which words have the main stress in the bold expression in each sentence.	Expressions like this often have this stress.
▪ ■ *As far as I'm concerned*, money is everything. ▪ ■ *As far as success is concerned*, it's important. ▪ ■ *When it comes to money*, I'm successful. ▪ ■ *In terms of money*, I'm pretty successful.	▪ ■ *As far as I know*, my friends are happy. **Stressing *I* means "it's only my view."** ▪ ■ *As far as I know*, they're happy.

A ◀)) CD 3.35 **Read and listen to the information above. Repeat the example sentences.**

B ◀)) CD 3.36 **Listen. Circle the stressed words in the bold expressions. Then listen and repeat.**

1. **As far as I can tell,** most of my friends are happy in terms of their social lives.
2. **As far as I'm concerned,** anyone can be happy. You just have to *choose* to be happy.
3. **When it comes to happiness,** it's probably much more important than being successful.
4. **As far as I know,** most successful people have worked very hard. They deserve their success.
5. **As far as I'm concerned,** there's no point being successful if you're not happy.
6. **As far as my friends are concerned,** they're all very ambitious in terms of their careers.

About you **C** Pair work **Discuss the sentences in Exercise B. Which views do you agree with?**

"Yeah. As far as I know, most of my friends are happy and enjoy what they're doing."

4 Unit 10, Lesson B Silent vowels

Notice how one vowel in each of these words is "silent" or very reduced.

traveling   family   business   interesting

A ◀)) CD 4.06 **Read and listen to the information above. Repeat the example words.**

B ◀)) CD 4.07 **Listen. Draw a line (/) through the silent vowel in the words in bold. Then listen again and repeat the questions.**

1. What's the most **interesting** place you've ever visited?
2. What's your **favorite** place to visit in your town or city?
3. What would your **preference** be: to stay at a friend's house or in a hotel?
4. When you go away, what's the most **valuable** thing you take with you?
5. Do you **generally** go away with your **family** or with your friends?
6. On **average**, how many trips a year do you take?
7. Do you know anyone who goes away on **business** a lot?
8. What's the best thing about **traveling**? And the worst?
9. What do you do in the **evenings** when you're not at work or in class?
10. Do you always go to the same place in your free time, or do you go to **different** places?

About you **C** Pair work **Take turns asking and answering the questions in Exercise B. Then find a new partner. Tell him or her your first partner's answers to the questions.**

Unit 11, Lesson C **Consonant groups**

> Notice that when two or more consonant sounds are together, one consonant sound
> (often *t, th, d,* or *k*) is sometimes not pronounced.*
>
> **In the middle of words**   **Across two words**
> I **asked my** parents.   I **don't know**.   I **just got** it.
> It **costs too** much.   It's a **gift for** you.   It's **next Saturday**.
> It was a few **months ago**.   It was a **gold bracelet**.   I always **send them** a card.
>
> *Grammatical endings like the *-s* or *-ed* of verbs are usually pronounced.

A CD 4.23 Read and listen to the information above. Repeat the example sentences.

B CD 4.24 Read these conversations. Look at the words in bold. Draw a line (/) through the
consonants that are not pronounced. Then listen, check, and repeat.

1. *A* What's the **best gift** you've ever received?
   B My parents gave me a **gold necklace**. They gave it to me **last May** for my graduation.
       It was the **most beautiful** gift I've ever gotten.

2. *A* Do you always buy your **best friends** a birthday card?
   B No way! It **costs too** much. Sometimes I **send them** an email.

3. *A* When was the **last time** you got a gift?
   B I **don't know**. Let's see . . . well, a few **months ago**. I **just got** some chocolates.

4. *A* Your birthday's **next Saturday**, isn't it? Do you know what you'll be getting?
   B Actually, it's **next Sunday**, but I've **asked my** parents not to buy me anything this year.

About
you **C** **Pair work** Practice the conversations in Exercise B. Practice again, giving your own answers.

 Unit 12, Lesson A **Stress and intonation**

> Notice how new information gets the main stress in a conversation. The voice goes up
> on the main stress and then falls or continues to rise.
>
> **Words already in the conversation are often**   **Contrasting ideas are often stressed.**
> **not stressed in the responses.**
>
> *A* My **sister** wants to study **math**.   *A* I'm really **bad** at **French**.
>
> *B* So is your sister **good** at math?   *B* Aren't you **good** at languages?
>
> *A* **Yeah,** she's **incredibly** good at math.   *A* **No!** I'm **terrible** at languages.

A CD 4.30 Read and listen to the information above. Repeat the example conversations.

B CD 4.31 Listen. The stressed words in the first lines are in bold. Circle the words with the main
stress in the responses. Then practice with a partner.

1. *A* I'm not very **good** at learning **languages**.
   B Really? Well, learning languages is difficult.
   A Yeah. It's extremely difficult.

2. *A* One of my **classmates** has a real **talent** for **music**.
   B I wish I had a talent for music!
   A Yeah. I can't even sing in tune.
   B Well, I can't sing in tune or play an instrument or anything.

1 **Objects with separable phrasal verbs**

- With separable phrasal verbs, you can put noun objects before or after the particle, but long noun objects generally go after the particle.
  *Don't forget to turn off **the TV**. / Don't forget to turn **the TV** off.*
  *Don't forget to turn off **the TV, the computer, and all the lights in the living room and kitchen.***

- Object pronouns (*me, you, him, it,* etc.) always go before the particle. However, indefinite pronouns (*something, anybody,* etc.) and possessive pronouns (*mine, yours,* etc.) can go after the particle.
  *My roommate borrowed my belt, and she never gave **it** back.*
  *She's always borrowing my stuff, and she never gives back **anything** / gives **anything** back.*
  *My room is dirty, but I won't clean **it** up unless you clean up **yours** / you clean **yours** up.*

About you   **Complete the sentences with the objects and verbs given. More than one answer may be possible. Then rewrite the sentences to make them true for you.**

1. Before I go to bed, I always _____ . (everything / put away)
2. If I'm late, I try hard not to _____ . (my parents and my sister / wake up)
3. When I get up, I always _____ first. (the television / turn on)
4. If I borrow something, I try to _____ as soon as possible. (it / give back)
5. I never leave things on the floor. I always _____ . (everything / pick up)
6. I don't _____ . (bottles, cans, or any food packaging / throw away)

2 **Phrasal verbs followed by the *-ing* form of the verb**

- You can use an *-ing* form after many phrasal verbs. The *-ing* form follows the particle.
  *I've almost given up **trying** to get along with my roommates. I may end up **moving** out.*

- Some verbs consist of a verb, a particle, and a preposition. The *-ing* form follows the preposition.
  *My brother never gets around to **doing** the dishes. He gets away with **leaving** them.*

> **Common errors**
>
> Don't use an infinitive or base form of the verb after a particle or preposition.
> *We're looking forward **to seeing** you.* (NOT ~~We're looking forward to see you.~~)

A **Rewrite the sentences. Replace the words in bold with a correct form of a phrasal verb in the box. Write the verb in parentheses in the correct form.**

end up   get around to   get out of   give up   keep on   look forward to   put off   take care of

1. My roommate never **finds the time** (do) any chores at the apartment.
2. He always **delays** (do) the dishes and says he'll do them later.
3. So I **finally** (do) the dishes all by myself.
4. He manages to **avoid** (shop) for food by going out of town on the weekends.
5. I have to **take responsibility for** (buy) all the groceries.
6. People tell me I should **continue** (try) to work things out with him.
7. Anyhow I've **stopped** (try) to talk to him about it.
8. I'm **excited about** (move) out of the apartment at the end of the semester.

B **Write about someone you know. Is he or she helpful around the house?**

More patterns with infinitives and *it* clauses

- You can use *too* before an adjective + infinitive, especially *late*, *young*, *early*, *busy*, *small*, *old*, *long*, *good*, *tired*, *easy*, *hard*, and *difficult*.
  It's never **too late** to learn new things.   I was **too young** to remember my grandmother.

- You can add *for* + person after the adjective, especially after *hard*, *difficult*, and *easy*.
  It's difficult / hard **for me** to make decisions.   It's not easy **for a lot of people** to raise children.

- You can use *to* or *for* + person with *interesting*, *fascinating*, and *important*.
  It's interesting **to me** / **for me** to watch parents with their children.
  It's important **to many people** / **for many people** to live near their families.

- People frequently use *not* with these adjectives beginning with *un-*, *in-*, or *im-*, especially in academic writing: *uncommon*, *impossible*, and *unusual*. The adjective can be followed directly by an infinitive or by *for* + person.
  It's **not uncommon** to feel sad when your children leave home to go to college.
  It's **not unusual** for families to argue about money.

A Rewrite these statements adding the ideas in parentheses.

1. Parents often put a lot of pressure on their kids. (It's not unusual.)
   <u>It's not unusual for parents to put a lot of pressure on their kids.</u>

2. Some parents let their kids have free time for themselves. (It's very important.)
   _____

3. Children often think that their parents are narrow-minded. (It's not uncommon.)
   _____

4. I couldn't understand my parents' views when I was younger. (It was difficult.)
   _____

5. Parents often can't understand why their children are fighting with each other. (It's not easy.)
   _____

6. I enjoy seeing how different families handle discipline. (It's always interesting.)
   _____

7. Brothers and sisters sometimes go on fighting even after they leave home. (It's not unusual.)
   _____

8. You should always apologize to a family member if you've had a fight. (It's never too late.)
   _____

9. Kids shouldn't move back in with their parents after they finish college. (It's probably not good.)
   _____

10. College graduates frequently can't find jobs, though. (It's sometimes too hard.)
    _____

About you

B Use these expressions to introduce five of your ideas about family life.

> It wasn't easy for me . . .   It's not uncommon for children . . .   It's not unusual for families . . .
> It's too difficult for me . . .   It's very important for parents . . .

Question forms in the passive

- In most passive questions, the auxiliary verb (*is*, *were*, *have*, etc.) or modal verb (*will*, *can*, etc.) comes before the subject.

Statement	Yes-No question	Information question
The population **is expected** to rise.	**Is** the population **expected** to rise?	When **is** it **expected** to rise?
The issue **is being discussed**.	**Is** the issue **being discussed**?	Where **is** it **being discussed**?
The idea **was developed** at Columbia.	**Was** the idea **developed** at Columbia?	Where **was** it **developed**?
Crops **have been grown** in water.	**Have** crops **been grown** in water?	How long **have** they **been grown** in water?
Water **will be recycled**.	**Will** water **be recycled**?	How **will** it **be recycled**?

- When the question word is the subject, the auxiliary or modal verb does not change position.
  Vertical farming **is going to be discussed** next week. → What**'s going to be discussed** next week?
  An expert in vertical farming **will be invited** to speak. → Who **will be invited** to speak?

- Information questions about the "doer" can end in *by*.
  Vertical farming **was developed by** Despommier. → Who **was** vertical farming **developed by**?

A Complete these *yes-no* questions in the passive for the responses given.

1. A ___Is the population expected___ to increase in the future?
   B Yes, the population is expected to increase by 3 to 4 billion people in the next 50 years.

2. A _____ to feed this population?
   B Yes, more food can definitely be produced, but it won't be easy.

3. A _____ to increase the food supply?
   B Actually, several methods have been developed. One is called vertical farming.

4. A _____ anywhere at the moment?
   B Yes, vertical farming is being used in a number of places. But the method is still experimental.

B Complete the information questions in the passive.

1. A How long ___have crops been grown in water___ ?
   B Crops have been grown in water since ancient times.

2. A What _____ ?
   B This method of farming is called hydroponics.

3. A Who _____ ?
   B Hydroponics was first used by the Egyptians, the Aztecs, and the Chinese in ancient times.

4. A Where _____ ?
   B Most hydroponic crops are grown in greenhouses.

5. A How _____ ?
   B Land can be conserved by building high-rise hydroponic greenhouses in urban areas.

6. A What kind of costs _____ ?
   B Transportation costs would be reduced by urban vertical farming.

① **Verb + object + infinitive**

- Many verbs follow the pattern of verb + object + infinitive: *advise, ask, encourage, expect, force, get (= persuade), invite, persuade, remind, tell, want, warn, would like.*
  My doctor **wants me to eat** less meat and fat.
  The government is **encouraging people to eat** more fruits and vegetables.
  BUT The government is **discouraging people from eating** too much fat.

- Notice the position of *not*.
  The doctor warned me **not** to eat too much fat.   He advised me **not** to go on any extreme diets.

> **Common errors**
>
> Do not use a *that* clause after the verb *want*.
> **I want all my friends to have** a healthy diet. (NOT ~~I want that all my friends have~~ . . .)

About
you

Unscramble these sentences. Then choose four sentences and rewrite them with your own ideas or information.

1. is encouraging / their eating habits / the government / to improve / people
   The government is encouraging people to improve their eating habits.
2. to pay / us / a special tax / the government / may force / on sugar-filled drinks
3. students / my college / is discouraging / from / energy drinks / drinking
4. during the school day / schools / unhealthy snacks / don't want / to eat / children
5. not / me / to eat / my doctor / too much junk food / advised
6. to eat / are always reminding / a good breakfast / my parents / me
7. me / to stop / has persuaded / my best friend / eating meat
8. is trying to get / my brother / some weight / to lose / me

② **More verb patterns**

- Some verbs can follow the pattern of verb + object + adjective. Examples are *make* and *keep*.
  Trying to stay healthy **keeps me busy**.
  Complicated instructions **make some diets hard** to follow.

- Verbs that express likes and dislikes can also follow this pattern. Examples are *like, would like, hate, prefer,* and *find*.
  I find some cheese too salty.   **I don't like my tea cold.**   **I prefer it really hot.**
  He **likes his fish baked** or **fried.**   He doesn't **like it raw.**

About
you

Complete these sentences with the appropriate form of a verb from the box. Then rewrite the sentences to make them true for you.

| find | keep | like | make | ✓ prefer |

1. My father hates eating raw vegetables. He __prefers__ his vegetables cooked.
2. I never drink coffee after noon. It _____ me awake at night.
3. I avoid eating pasta for lunch. It _____ me sleepy all afternoon.
4. My brother eats a lot of junk food. He _____ a healthy diet very boring.
5. A friend of mine puts chili peppers in all her cooking. She _____ her food hot and spicy.

Unit 9, Lesson A   *Grammar extra*

 Singular or plural verbs with determiners

> • Use a singular verb with *each*, *every*, and *neither* + countable noun or the pronoun *one*.
> *Each child / Every child* **is** unique and special, and *each one / every one* **needs** individual attention.
> *I have two children, and neither child* **has** any interest in sports. Neither one **plays** sports.
>
> • Use a singular verb with *no* + singular countable or uncountable noun. Use a plural verb with *no* + plural noun.
> *No success* **comes** easily.   *No job* **is** perfect.   Unfortunately, no good jobs **are** available right now.
>
> • People mostly use a plural verb after *neither of* and *none of*. In formal writing, people use a singular verb.
> Informal: *Neither of my parents* **have studied** English. None of their friends **have learned** English, either.
> Formal: *Neither of my parents* **has studied** English. None of their friends **has learned** English, either.

About
you

Circle the correct verb in each sentence. Sometimes both forms can be correct. Then choose three sentences and rewrite them with your own ideas or information.

1. Both of my brothers **has** / (**have**) finished college, but neither one **has** / **have** found a job yet. No companies **is** / **are** hiring people right now.
2. All successful people **knows** / **know** that every failure **presents** / **present** an opportunity.
3. I've had two jobs. Neither of them **was** / **were** perfect, but each one **was** / **were** interesting.
4. All of my friends **is** / **are** focused on their work. None of them **wants** / **want** to get married.
5. Neither of my parents **wants** / **want** me to be an entrepreneur. Both of them **has** / **have** advised me to study for a profession.
6. No job **is** / **are** ever completely secure. Every employee **needs** / **need** to save money "for a rainy day."

② Determiners with and without *of*

> • You can use *all*, *each*, *every*, *both*, *neither*, *some*, *a few*, *several*, *many*, and *most* before a noun.
> **Every job** is different. **A few jobs** seem easy, but **most jobs** are challenging in some way.
>
> • When most of these determiners are followed by another determiner + noun or by an object pronoun, add *of*. With *all* and *both*, *of* is optional before a noun. *A lot of* always includes *of*. After *every*, use *one of*.
> **Each of my children** is different. **Each of them** has a different job, but **every one of** them is happy.
> **All (of) the people** at work want to do well. **All of us** work hard. **A lot of people / us** work weekends.
> **Both (of) my parents** have interesting careers. **Neither of them** wants / want to retire.
>
> • Use *no* before a noun. Use *none of* + determiner + noun or *none of* + object pronoun.
> **No employees** are unhappy. **None of the employees / them** is / are unhappy.

About
you

Complete the sentences with the words in the box. Add *of* if necessary. In some, more than one word is possible. Then rewrite the sentences with your own ideas or information.

all	both	each	every	every one	most	neither	no	none

1. I have five close friends, and __all of__ them have jobs. _____ them is unemployed.
2. _____ jobs require training, but for my current job, _____ formal training was necessary.
3. _____ student in my English course is serious, and _____ them ever miss a class.
4. _____ my parents enjoy being retired. _____ them wish they could keep on working.
5. _____ the people in my family love sports, but _____ us plays a different sport.
6. I'm not married, but _____ my sisters are. _____ sister has any children yet, though.

Verbs followed by an *-ing* form or an infinitive

- Use *forget*, *remember*, and *regret* + an *-ing* form to mean "remember / forget / regret that someone did something." You can also use these verbs with an infinitive to mean "remember / forget / regret something that someone needs or needed to do."
  *I'll never **forget going up** to get my college diploma. BUT I **forgot to shake** the president's hand.*
  *I **remember thanking** my professor as I left. BUT I always **remember to say** thank you.*

- You can use *stop* and *try* + an *-ing* form or an infinitive, but they have different meanings.
  *I've **stopped drinking** soda. (= I don't drink it now.)*
  *BUT I **stopped to pick up** some fruit juice at the store. (**to** = in order to)*
  *I **tried giving up** coffee for a whole year, but then I started drinking it again. (**try** = experiment with)*
  *BUT I **tried to give up** sweets, but I just couldn't do it. (**try** = try without success)*

About you

Complete this anecdote with the correct form of the verbs given. Then write a short anecdote about something that happened to you.

I'll never forget <u>hiking</u> (hike) through the Amazon rain forest. It had been my dream to go there. I was on a tour and at one point, I stopped _____ (get) some pictures of tropical birds. After a while, I couldn't hear the voices of the other hikers, so I stopped _____ (take) pictures and tried _____ (catch up with) the group. Unfortunately, I couldn't find the path. I tried _____ (yell) for help several times, but no one heard me. I looked for my GPS device but realized I had forgotten _____ (put) it in my pack that day. I hadn't remembered _____ (bring) my map, either. I remember _____ (think) that I'd never find my group again. Luckily, our guide stopped _____ (count) the hikers and noticed I was missing. He led the whole group back to find me. He was very annoyed, and I have to say I regretted _____ (take) those pictures. My happiest moment turned into my scariest.

② **Verbs of perception + object + base form or *-ing* form**

- After the verbs *feel*, *see*, *watch*, *notice*, and *hear*, you can use an object + the base form of a verb to describe a complete event.
  *I **watched** my friends **leave** the restaurant. I **heard** someone **say**, "See you soon."*
  *I **saw** my sister **call** a taxi and **felt** her **take** my arm and **guide** me to it.*

- You can also use an object + an *-ing* form after these verbs to describe an event in progress or an event that takes place over a longer period of time.
  *I **heard** people **singing**. I went in the room and **saw** all my friends **standing** around the piano.*

A Rewrite these sentences using the verbs of perception given.

1. Some strange things were happening as I walked up to my house. (noticed)
   I noticed some strange things happening as I walked up to my house.
2. Someone turned off the lights in the living room. (saw)
3. Someone was closing the curtains. (noticed)
4. People were talking to each other softly. (could hear)
5. Somebody yelled "Surprise!" when I walked into the living room. (heard)
6. Several people were holding up a big birthday cake. (saw)

About you

B Write an anecdote about a happy moment. Use verbs of perception.

Reported speech: verbs and pronouns

- When you report things people say, you may need to change the pronouns in the reported sentence.
  *"**I** left **my** camera on the plane."* → *Karen said that **she** had left **her** camera on the plane.*
  *"**We**'re happy to carry **your** bags."* → *The guides said that **they** were happy to carry **my/our** bags.*

- The verb in the reported sentence often "shifts back." You do not always need to change the simple past or past continuous. The past perfect does not change.
  *"I'm really **enjoying** the trip."* → *Rob said that he **was** really **enjoying** the trip.*
  *"I **don't like** the hotel, though."* → *He told me that he **didn't like** the hotel, though.*
  *"I **wasn't feeling** well."* → *He explained that he **hadn't been feeling** well. (OR **wasn't feeling**)*
  *"I **met up with** an old friend."* → *He said that he **had met up with / met** an old friend.*
  *"I**'ve seen** some amazing things."* → *He told me that he**'d seen** some amazing things.*
  *"I **hadn't been** there before."* → *He said that he **hadn't been** there before.*

A Report the things that people said after a trip. There may be more than one correct answer.

1. Karen: "I'm planning to go back to Florida. I've never enjoyed a vacation so much!"
   Karen said _____ and _____ .

2. Joe and Sue: "The airline made us check our luggage and lost it. We've never had that happen before."
   Joe and Sue said _____ . They said _____ .

3. Sandra: "I met my boyfriend on vacation. He was sitting next to me on the plane."
   Sandra told me _____ . She said _____ .

4. Ana: "I had a great time in India. I hadn't been there before."
   Ana said _____ . She said _____ .

5. Guy: "My mom didn't like the food. That surprised me."
   He said _____ . He said _____ .

About
you

B Write five sentences about trips you've taken in the past, and give them to a partner. Report your partner's comments.

❷ Reported speech: time and place expressions

- Time and place expressions often change in the reported sentence.

next week → *the following week* or *the week after*	*this morning* → *that morning*	*here* → *there*
tomorrow → *the following day* or *the day after*	*today* → *that day*	
yesterday → *the previous day* or *the day before*	*now* → *then*	
last year → *the year before*	*then* → *then* or *after that*	

  *"We're going to the beach **this** morning."* → *He said they were going to the beach **that** morning.*
  *"**Yesterday** we went to a farm."* → *He said that they had gone to a farm **the day before**.*

Report this extract from Rona's blog. Rewrite the sentences.

Another day in Tuscany . . . We're eating breakfast outside this morning. We couldn't do that yesterday because there was a huge thunderstorm. It's beautiful here. This afternoon we're going to a farm and we're going to pick olives. Then we're going to learn how they make olive oil. Tomorrow we're visiting our friends. We saw them last year back home. It'll be the first time we've been to their home in Italy. Then next week we're going to drive to the coast. We're having a fabulous time!

Rona said that they were eating breakfast outside that morning.

❶ Reported speech: other reporting verbs

- You can use different verbs to report the things people say, especially in writing. To report statements, you can use verbs such as *add*, *answer*, *claim*, *complain*, *comment*, *confirm*, *explain*, *inform*, *mention*, *predict*, *promise*, *remark*, *remind*, *reply*, *say*, *state*, and *tell*.

  With *add*, *answer*, *claim*, *comment*, *confirm*, *predict*, *remark*, *reply*, and *state*, use a *that* clause.
  "The flight's at 8:00 a.m. You should check in by 7:00 a.m."
  *She **confirmed** (that) the flight was at 8:00 a.m. and **added** (that) we should check in by 7:00 a.m.*

  With *inform*, *remind*, and *tell*, use an indirect object and a *that* clause.
  *"The flight's full." The agent **informed** me (that) the flight was full.*

  With *comment*, *complain*, *explain*, *mention*, *say*, and *reply*, you can use a *that* clause or *to* + person + a *that* clause.
  *"My room is noisy." I **complained** (to the receptionist) (that) my room was noisy.*

- To report questions, you can use *ask*, *inquire* (more formal), *want to know*, and *wonder*.
  *"Are you leaving?" He **wanted to know** if I was leaving. / He **inquired** whether I was leaving.*

- To report instructions, you can use *advise*, *instruct*, *order*, *persuade*, *remind*, and *warn*.
  *"Don't forget your hat." She **advised** me not to forget my hat. / She **reminded** me to take my hat.*

Complete the sentences so they have a similar meaning. Use the words given.

1. The tour agent said to us, "Don't go off the trail." He also said, "Take some food."
   The tour agent _____ (warned) the trail. He also _____ (reminded) some food.
2. The check-in agent asked me, "Are you traveling alone?" and "Did you pack your bags yourself?"
   The check-in agent _____ (wanted to know). She also _____ (inquired).
3. The tour guide said, "Drink plenty of water." He said, "It will be a tough walk."
   The tour guide _____ (advised). He _____ (added).
4. One passenger said, "The flight's been delayed for four hours. We should get a voucher for a free meal."
   One passenger _____ (complained). He also _____ (mentioned).

❷ Reported speech: reporting verb forms

- When the reporting verb is in the present tense, the verb often does not need to "shift back" because the information may still be true or relevant to the present time.
  *"**I'm having** a great time."* ➔ *She says she**'s having** a great time.*

- People often use the past continuous to report news. You can use the present tense or the present perfect in the reported speech if the information is still true.
  "The airlines have raised their prices." ➔ *He **was saying** the airlines have raised their prices.*

A Imagine you have just heard these comments. Report each one. Start with the words given.

1. "I'm traveling on business right now. I'm sitting in the airport in Beijing." *He says . . .*
2. "The flights are delayed because of the snow. We'll be arriving late." *She says . . .*
3. "I had a great trip. I saw dolphins and some amazing birds." *He was saying . . .*
4. "The government is promoting tourism. They don't want to lose tourist dollars." *She was saying . . .*

About you

B Write five pieces of news. Then give them to a partner. Report your partner's news.

More on relative clauses

• A defining relative clause defines or gives essential information about a noun. The sentence needs the relative clause to complete its meaning.	*Spring is the time **when many people get married**. The hotel **where my parents had their reception** closed. I have an uncle **whose marriage was arranged**.*
• A non-defining relative clause gives extra information about a noun. The sentence has a complete meaning without the relative clause. Notice the commas.	*People like to get married in the spring, **when it's warmer**. There was a garden, **where the photos were taken**. He had strict parents, **whose aim was to find him a bride**.*

Common errors

Do not use *which* for possession before a noun.
*We went to a hotel, **whose** name I've forgotten.* (NOT ~~which name~~ . . .)

Rewrite each pair of sentences as one sentence. Start with the words given. Use relative clauses with *when, where*, or *whose*. Add commas where necessary.

1. I have several friends. Their wedding ceremonies were outside.
   I have several friends *whose wedding ceremonies were outside.*

2. The hotel has just appeared in a bridal magazine. We got married there.
   The hotel _____

3. The best season to get married is winter. The trees are covered in snow.
   The best season to get married is winter _____

4. I have conservative parents. Their main concern is to find a husband for me.
   I have conservative parents _____

5. After the ceremony, we went to a Japanese restaurant. We ate sushi.
   After the ceremony, _____

② Prepositions in relative clauses

• In spoken or informal English, relative clauses can end with a preposition.	*I married a co-worker who I'd shared an office **with**. We met at a golf club, which we both belonged **to**.*
• In formal English, prepositions can start a relative clause. Notice the use of *whom* for people and *which* (not *that*) for things.	*I married a co-worker **with whom** I'd shared an office. We met at a golf club, **to which** we both belonged.*
• You can often rephrase a relative clause that ends with a preposition of location by using *where*.	*That's the place that we went **to** for our photos. OR That's the place **where** we went for our photos.*
• A preposition of location can also start the relative clause in more formal English.	*The Royal is the hotel **in / at** which we stayed. OR The Royal is the hotel we stayed **in / at**. (less formal)*

Rewrite the sentences. Make the comments in 1–3 less formal. Sometimes there is more than one answer. Sentences 4–6 are extracts from a letter of complaint. Make them more formal.

1. The Ritz is the restaurant to which we are going for the rehearsal dinner.
2. I want to marry a person with whom I share a lot of interests.
3. My wife and I met at a homeless shelter at which we both volunteered.
4. The dinner at the reception, which we had paid a lot of money for, was cold.
5. We complained to the hotel manager, who we had an argument with.
6. The question which we want an answer to is, "Why was the meal cold?"

More on verb + direct object + prepositional phrase

• With these verbs, use *for* in the prepositional phrase: *bake, buy, cook, draw, find, make,* and *paint*.	*Will you bake a cake **for** me?* *I'm painting a picture **for** my father.*
• With most other verbs, use *to*: *give, hand, lend, offer, owe, pay, read, send, show,* and *write*.	*I didn't send a gift **to** him this year.* *We handed all our money **to** the clerk.*
• With *bring* and *take*, you can use *for* or *to*, but the meaning is different.	*I've brought some flowers **for** you.* (= They're a gift.) *Can I borrow your laptop? I'll bring it back **to** you later.*

About you

Rewrite the sentences using a direct object + prepositional phrase. Then use the ideas to write true sentences of your own.

1. I always bake my sister a cake on her birthday.
2. I never give my friends money. I prefer to hand them a nicely wrapped gift.
3. When friends invite you for dinner, it's nice to offer your host a small gift.
4. On special occasions, I'll often cook my family a nice meal.
5. If you want to give a friend who has everything a gift, a magazine subscription is a good idea.
6. When I get greeting cards, I always show my family the messages.
7. When I have to send someone a gift in the mail, I always choose something small.
8. I once made a friend an unusual gift. I drew him a picture of his cat.
9. My parents once bought me an underwater camera for my birthday.

 Passive sentences

- In the passive, either the indirect object or the direct object can become the subject of the sentence.
- Compare this active sentence with the two passive sentences below.

subject	active verb	indirect object	direct object
My aunt	*gave*	*me*	*this ring.*

Indirect object as subject	Direct object as subject
I *was given this ring (by my aunt).* This pattern is more common.	**This ring** *was given to me (by my aunt).* This pattern is less common and often more formal.

Rewrite these sentences in the passive form. Start with the words given.

1. The school gave us certificates when we completed the course. *We . . .*
   We were given certificates (by the school) when we completed the course.
2. My father's company gave him a clock when he retired. *A clock . . .*
3. Someone sent my sister a gift card for her birthday. *My sister . . .*
4. One of my friends owes me a lot of money. *I . . .*
5. Someone handed me a microphone so I could make a speech at my party. *A microphone . . .*
6. My mother always gave us a piece of jewelry for our birthdays. *We . . .*

① *well* + adjective

- You can use *well* before the adjectives below. It means "very" or "very much." Add a hyphen when *well* + adjective comes before a noun.
  I'm **well aware** of my abilities. I'm **well educated** and **well trained**.
  I'm also a **well-organized** and **well-informed** person.
  He wasn't **well prepared** for the exam. He was **well short of** the 90 percent he needed.

- You can use *well* in a number of fixed expressions, e.g., *well off, well known, well thought-out, well behaved, well written,* and *well dressed*.
  My teacher said my poem was **well written**. He said it was a **well-written** piece.
  She must be very **well off** now that she's a **well-known** architect.

About you | Complete the sentences with the expressions in the box. Do you agree? Write sentences expressing your own views.

| well educated | well informed | well-known | well off | well-organized | well prepared |
| well thought-out | well-written |

1. It's important to have a _____ work space. You can save a lot of time looking for things.
2. Many people aren't very _____ these days. They don't read the news or know what's going on.
3. You should be _____ before any interview. Find out what you can about the job first.
4. People often say that students can't produce a _____ essay or one that's _____ .
5. To be _____ , you need to learn art, music, and languages – not just math and science.
6. People who are _____ , have to work very hard. Isn't that a _____ fact?

② Adverb and adjective collocations

- Certain adverbs are commonly used with certain adjectives. Here are some common combinations.
  = 100 percent   **completely:** *different, new, unknown, separate, safe, unrealistic*
                         entirely: *different, new, sure, possible, clear, appropriate, accurate*
                         totally: *different, wrong, false, honest, convinced, unacceptable, irrelevant*
  = nearly 100 percent   **virtually:** *impossible, unknown, identical, unchanged, nonexistent*
  = very   **highly:** *qualified, unlikely, effective, skilled, respected, educated, intelligent*
  = in many places   **widely:** *available, known, accepted, respected*

A Complete the sentences with an adverb from above. There may be more than one answer.

1. Being good with people is a _____ different kind of intelligence from being good at math.
2. Smart people aren't all _____ educated. It's _____ possible to be smart and uneducated.
3. I'm not _____ convinced that intelligence is knowing lots of facts. It's _____ wrong.
4. Latin is _____ nonexistent in schools now. It's _____ irrelevant in today's world.
5. It's _____ impossible to have every type of intelligence. In fact, it's _____ unknown.
6. You have to be _____ intelligent or _____ qualified to be a _____ respected person.
7. It's a _____ known fact that listening to music can help children with their math ability.

About you | **B** Do you agree with the statements above? Write sentences expressing your own views.

1. I agree. They require totally different kinds of skills. I think . . .

Patterns with comparatives

- You can use nouns, pronouns, or clauses after *than* and *as*. Notice the verb forms in the clauses.

Bryan cycles faster than **his teammates**.	*They don't cycle as fast as* **Bryan**.
He's faster than **them**.	*They're not as fast as* **him**.
He's faster than **they are**.	*They're not as fast as* **he is**.
He cycles faster than **they do**.	*They don't cycle as fast as* **he does**.
He trains harder than **he did**.	*He didn't use to train as hard as* **he does** *now*.
He's faster than **he used to be**. */* **he was**.	*He's cycling further than* **he used to**. */* **he did**.
Nurdan practices less often than **she should**.	*She plays as often as* **she can**.
She's improved more slowly than **she hoped**.	*She hasn't improved as much as* **she'd like**.

> **Common errors**
>
> Use *than*, not *that*, in comparisons.
> *He's faster* **than** *his teammates.* (NOT *. . . faster* ~~*that his teammates*~~.)

About you

Complete the second sentences. Sometimes more than one option is possible. Then use the topic of each sentence above to write your own true sentences.

1. I'm better than my classmates at mental math. They're not as good _____ .
2. My sister reads faster than anyone in the family. We can't read as fast _____ .
3. My English hasn't improved as much as I'd like. I'm not as fluent _____ .
4. I'm training much harder this year for the marathon. I now run much faster _____ .
5. Both my parents are learning Italian. But my father doesn't practice as often _____ .
6. My friend Ana understands people really well. My other friends aren't as understanding _____ .
7. One guy in our class can play the guitar really well. No one can play it as well _____ .
8. My brother's swimming has improved. He's more confident _____ .

❷ More patterns with comparatives

- Comparatives are often repeated with *and* to talk about changing situations.
  Work just gets **busier and busier***. I'm finding it* **more and more difficult** *to catch up.*

- Comparatives are often used in the pattern *the* + comparative, *the* + comparative to show the effect of one event on another. In this pattern, *more* is often an adverb.
  The harder *you practice an instrument,* **the better** *you get.* (= If you practice harder, you get better.)
  The more *I thought about it,* **the more nervous** */* **the less confident** *I'd feel.*

A **Rewrite the sentences starting with the words given.**

1. If you read more, you learn more. *The more . . .*   The more you read, the more you learn.
2. If you do something, you like it better. *The more . . .*
3. If you work hard, you feel happy. *The harder . . .*
4. As you get older, life becomes more rewarding. *The older . . .*
5. If you practice a skill more, it becomes easier. *The more . . .*
6. Getting into college is increasingly difficult. *It's getting more and . . .*
7. Beating records in most sports is getting harder. *It's becoming harder and . . .*
8. When I find out more about politics, I like it less. *The more . . .*

About you

B **Do you agree with the sentences above? Write your own view and give examples.**

Illustration credits

Photography credits

Text credits

Corpus

Development of this publication has made use of the Cambridge English Corpus (CEC). The CEC is a computer database of contemporary spoken and written English, which currently stands at over one billion words. It includes British English, American English and other varieties of English. It also includes the Cambridge Learner Corpus, developed in collaboration with the University of Cambridge ESOL Examinations. Cambridge University Press has built up the CEC to provide evidence about language use that helps to produce better language teaching materials.